The Economist

Xenophon

Translated by Henry G. Dakyns

DODO PRESS

Xenophon the Athenian was born 431 B. C. He was a pupil of Socrates. He marched with the Spartans, and was exiled from Athens. Sparta gave him land and property in Scillus, where he lived for many years before having to move once more, to settle in Corinth. He died in 354 B. C.

The Economist records Socrates and Critobulus in a talk about profitable estate management, and a lengthy recollection by Socrates of Ischomachus' discussion of the same topic.

THE ECONOMIST[1]

A Treatise on the Science of the Household in the form of a Dialogue

INTERLOCUTORS Socrates and Critobulus

At Chapter VII. a prior discussion held between Socrates and Ischomachus is introduced: On the life of a "beautiful and good" man.

In these chapters (vii. -xxi.) Socrates is represented by the author as repeating for the benefit of Critobulus and the rest certain conversations which he had once held with the beautiful and good Ischomachus on the essentials of economy. It was a tete-a-tete discussion, and in the original Greek the remarks of the two speakers are denoted by such phrases as {ephe o 'Iskhomakhos—ephen egio}—"said (he) Ischomachus, " "said I" (Socrates). To save the repetition of expressions tedious in English, I have, whenever it seemed help to do so, ventured to throw parts of the reported conversations into dramatic form, inserting "Isch. " "Soc. " in the customary way to designate the speakers; but these, it must be borne in mind, are merely "asides" to the reader, who will not forget that Socrates is the narrator throughout—speaking of himself as "I, " and of Ischomachus as "he, " or by his name. — Translator's note, addressed to the English reader.

The Economist

I

I once heard him[2] discuss the topic of economy[3] after the following manner. Addressing Critobulus, [4] he said: Tell me, Critobulus, is "economy, " like the words "medicine, " "carpentry, " "building, " "smithying, " "metal-working, " and so forth, the name of a particular kind of knowledge or science?

[1] By "economist" we now generally understand "policital economist, " but the use of the word as referring to domestic economy, the subject matter of the treatise, would seem to be legitimate.

[2] "The master. "

[3] Lit. "the management of a household and estate. " See Plat. "Rep. " 407 B; Aristot. "Eth. N." v. 6; "Pol. " i. 3.

[4] See "Mem. " I. iii. 8; "Symp. " p. 292.

Crit. Yes, I think so.

Soc. And as, in the case of the arts just named, we can state the proper work or function of each, can we (similarly) state the proper work and function of economy?

Crit. It must, I should think, be the business of the good economist[5] at any rate to manage his own house or estate well.

[5] Or, "manager of a house or estate. "

Soc. And supposing another man's house to be entrusted to him, he would be able, if he chose, to manage it as skilfully as his own, would he not? since a man who is skilled in carpentry can work as well for another as for himself: and this ought to be equally true of the good economist?

Crit. Yes, I think so, Socrates.

Soc. Then there is no reason why a proficient in this art, even if he does not happen to possess wealth of his own, should not be paid a

The Economist

salary for managing a house, just as he might be paid for building one?

Crit. None at all: and a large salary he would be entitled to earn if, after paying the necessary expenses of the estate entrusted to him, he can create a surplus and improve the property.

Soc. Well! and this word "house, " what are we to understand by it? the domicile merely? or are we to include all a man's possessions outside the actual dwelling-place? [6]

[6] Lit. "is it synonymous with dwelling-place, or is all that a man possesses outside his dwelling-place part of his house or estate? "

Crit. Certainly, in my opinion at any rate, everything which a man has got, even though some portion of it may lie in another part of the world from that in which he lives, [7] forms part of his estate.

[7] Lit. "not even in the same state or city. "

Soc. "Has got"? but he may have got enemies?

Crit. Yes, I am afraid some people have got a great many.

Soc. Then shall we say that a man's enemies form part of his possessions?

Crit. A comic notion indeed! that some one should be good enough to add to my stock of enemies, and that in addition he should be paid for his kind services.

Soc. Because, you know, we agreed that a man's estate was identical with his possessions?

Crit. Yes, certainly! the good part of his possessions; but the evil portion! no, I thank you, that I do not call part of a man's possessions.

Soc. As I understand, you would limit the term to what we may call a man's useful or advantageous possessions?

Crit. Precisely; if he has things that injure him, I should regard these rather as a loss than as wealth.

The Economist

Soc. It follows apparently that if a man purchases a horse and does not know how to handle him, but each time he mounts he is thrown and sustains injuries, the horse is not part of his wealth?

Crit. Not, if wealth implies weal, certainly.

Soc. And by the same token land itself is no wealth to a man who so works it that his tillage only brings him loss?

Crit. True; mother earth herself is not a source of wealth to us if, instead of helping us to live, she helps us to starve.

Soc. And by a parity of reasoning, sheep and cattle may fail of being wealth if, through want of knowledge how to treat them, their owner loses by them; to him at any rate the sheep and the cattle are not wealth?

Crit. That is the conclusion I draw.

Soc. It appears, you hold to the position that wealth consists of things which benefit, while things which injure are not wealth?

Crit. Just so.

Soc. The same things, in fact, are wealth or not wealth, according as a man knows or does not know the use to make of them? To take an instance, a flute may be wealth to him who is sufficiently skilled to play upon it, but the same instrument is no better than the stones we tread under our feet to him who is not so skilled . ... unless indeed he chose to sell it?

Crit. That is precisely the conclusion we should come to. [8] To persons ignorant of their use[9] flutes are wealth as saleable, but as possessions not for sale they are no wealth at all; and see, Socrates, how smoothly and consistently the argument proceeds, [10] since it is admitted that things which benefit are wealth. The flutes in question unsold are not wealth, being good for nothing: to become wealth they must be sold.

[8] Reading {tout auto}, or if {tout au} with Sauppe, transl. "Yes, that is another position we may fairly subscribe to."

[9] i. e. "without knowledge of how to use them."

[10] Or, "our discussion marches on all-fours, as it were."

Yes! (rejoined Socrates), presuming the owner knows how to sell them; since, supposing again he were to sell them for something which he does not know how to use, [11] the mere selling will not transform them into wealth, according to your argument.

[11] Reading {pros touto o}, or if {pros touton, os}, transl. "to a man who did not know how to use them."

Crit. You seem to say, Socrates, that money itself in the pockets of a man who does not know how to use it is not wealth?

Soc. And I understand you to concur in the truth of our proposition so far: wealth is that, and that only, whereby a man may be benefited. Obviously, if a man used his money to buy himself a mistress, to the grave detriment of his body and soul and whole estate, how is that particular money going to benefit him now? What good will he extract from it?

Crit. None whatever, unless we are prepared to admit that hyoscyamus, [12] as they call it, is wealth, a poison the property of which is to drive those who take it mad.

[12] "A dose of henbane, 'hogs'-bean, ' so called." Diosc. 4. 69; 6. 15; Plut. "Demetr." xx. (Clough, v. 114).

Soc. Let money then, Critobulus, if a man does not know how to use it aright—let money, I say, be banished to the remote corners of the earth rather than be reckoned as wealth. [13] But now, what shall we say of friends? If a man knows how to use his friends so as to be benefited by them, what of these?

[13] Or, "then let it be relegated . ... and there let it lie in the category of non-wealth."

Crit. They are wealth indisputably, and in a deeper sense than cattle are, if, as may be supposed, they are likely to prove of more benefit to a man than wealth of cattle.

Soc. It would seem, according to your argument, that the foes of a man's own household after all may be wealth to him, if he knows how to turn them to good account? [14]

The Economist

[14] Vide supra.

Crit. That is my opinion, at any rate.

Soc. It would seem, it is the part of a good economist[15] to know how to deal with his own or his employer's foes so as to get profit out of them?

[15] "A good administrator of an estate."

Crit. Most emphatically so.

Soc. In fact, you need but use your eyes to see how many private persons, not to say crowned heads, do owe the increase of their estates to war.

Crit. Well, Socrates, I do not think, so far, the argument could be improved on; [16] but now comes a puzzle. What of people who have got the knowledge and the capital[17] required to enhance their fortunes, if only they will put their shoulders to the wheel; and yet, if we are to believe our senses, that is just the one thing they will not do, and so their knowledge and accomplishments are of no profit to them? Surely in their case also there is but one conclusion to be drawn, which is, that neither their knowledge nor their possessions are wealth.

[16] Or, "Thanks, Socrates. Thus far the statement of the case would seem to be conclusive—but what are we to make of this? Some people . .. "

[17] Lit. "the right kinds of knowledge and the right starting- points."

Soc. Ah! I see, Critobulus, you wish to direct the discussion to the topic of slaves?

Crit. No indeed, I have no such intention—quite the reverse. I want to talk about persons of high degree, of right noble family[18] some of them, to do them justice. These are the people I have in my mind's eye, gifted with, it may be, martial or, it may be, civil accomplishments, which, however, they refuse to exercise, for the very reason, as I take it, that they have no masters over them.

[18] "Eupatrids."

Soc. No masters over them! but how can that be if, in spite of their prayers for prosperity and their desire to do what will bring them good, they are still so sorely hindered in the exercise of their wills by those that lord it over them?

Crit. And who, pray, are these lords that rule them and yet remain unseen?

Soc. Nay, not unseen; on the contrary, they are very visible. And what is more, they are the basest of the base, as you can hardly fail to note, if at least you believe idleness and effeminacy and reckless negligence to be baseness. Then, too, there are other treacherous beldames giving themselves out to be innocent pleasures, to wit, dicings and profitless associations among men. [19] These in the fulness of time appear in all their nakedness even to them that are deceived, showing themselves that they are after all but pains tricked out and decked with pleasures. These are they who have the dominion over those you speak of and quite hinder them from every good and useful work.

[19] Or, "frivolous society."

Crit. But there are others, Socrates, who are not hindered by these indolences—on the contrary, they have the most ardent disposition to exert themselves, and by every means to increase their revenues; but in spite of all, they wear out their substance and are involved in endless difficulties. [20]

[20] Or, "become involved for want of means."

Soc. Yes, for they too are slaves, and harsh enough are their taskmasters; slaves are they to luxury and lechery, intemperance and the wine-cup along with many a fond and ruinous ambition. These passions so cruelly belord it over the poor soul whom they have got under their thrall, that so long as he is in the heyday of health and strong to labour, they compel him to fetch and carry and lay at their feet the fruit of his toils, and to spend it on their own heart's lusts; but as soon as he is seen to be incapable of further labour through old age, they leave him to his gray hairs and misery, and turn to seize on other victims. [21] Ah! Critobulus, against these must we wage ceaseless war, for very freedom's sake, no less than if they were armed warriors endeavouring to make us their slaves. Nay, foemen in war, it must be granted, especially when of fair and noble type, have many times ere now proved benefactors to those they have enslaved. By dint of chastening, they have forced the vanquished to become better men and to lead more tranquil lives in future. [22] But these despotic queens never cease to plague and torment their victims in body and soul and substance until their sway is ended.

[21] "To use others as their slaves."

[22] Lit. "Enemies for the matter of that, when, being beautiful and good, they chance to have enslaved some other, have ere now in many an instance chastened and compelled the vanquished to be better and to live more easily for the rest of time."

The Economist

II

The conersation was resumed by Critobulus, and on this wise. He said: I think I take your meaning fully, Socrates, about these matters; and for myself, examining my heart, I am further satisfied, I have sufficient continence and self-command in those respects. So that if you will only advise me on what I am to do to improve my estate, I flatter myself I shall not be hindered by those despotic dames, as you call them. Come, do not hesitate; only tender me what good advice you can, and trust me I will follow it. But perhaps, Socrates, you have already passed sentence on us—we are rich enough already, and not in need of any further wealth?

Soc. It is to myself rather, if I may be included in your plural "we, " that I should apply the remark. I am not in need of any further wealth, if you like. I am rich enough already, to be sure. But you, Critobulus, I look upon as singularly poor, and at times, upon my soul, I feel a downright compassion for you.

At this view of the case, Critobulus fell to laughing outright, retorting: And pray, Socrates, what in the name of fortune do you suppose our respective properties would fetch in the market, yours and mine?

If I could find a good purchaser (he answered), I suppose the whole of my effects, including the house in which I live, might very fairly realise five minae[1] (say twenty guineas). Yours, I am positively certain, would fetch at the lowest more than a hundred times that sum.

[1] 5 x L4:1:3. See Boeckh, "P. E. A. " [Bk. i. ch. xx.], p. 109 f. (Eng. ed.)

Crit. And with this estimate of our respective fortunes, can you still maintain that you have no need of further wealth, but it is I who am to be pitied for my poverty?

Soc. Yes, for my property is amply sufficient to meet my wants, whereas you, considering the parade you are fenced about with, and the reputation you must needs live up to, would be barely well off, I take it, if what you have already were multiplied by three.

Pray, how may that be? Critobulus asked.

Why, first and foremost (Socrates explained), I see you are called upon to offer many costly sacrifices, failing which, I take it, neither gods nor men would tolerate you; and, in the next place, you are bound to welcome numerous foreigners as guests, and to entertain them handsomely; thirdly, you must feast your fellow-citizens and ply them with all sorts of kindness, or else be cut adrift from your supporters. [2] Furthermore, I perceive that even at present the state enjoins upon you various large contributions, such as the rearing of studs, [3] the training of choruses, the superintendence of gymnastic schools, or consular duties, [4] as patron of resident aliens, and so forth; while in the event of war you will, I am aware, have further obligations laid upon you in the shape of pay[5] to carry on the triearchy, ship money, and war taxes[6] so onerous, you will find difficulty in supporting them. Remissness in respect of any of these charges will be visited upon you by the good citizens of Athens no less strictly than if they caught you stealing their own property. But worse than all, I see you fondling the notion that you are rich. Without a thought or care how to increase your revenue, your fancy lightly turns to thoughts of love, [7] as if you had some special license to amuse yourselef. . ... That is why I pity and compassionate you, fearing lest some irremediable mischief overtake you, and you find yourself in desperate straits. As for me, if I ever stood in need of anything, I am sure you know I have friends who would assist me. They would make some trifling contribution—trifling to themselves, I mean—and deluge my humble living with a flood of plenty. But your friends, albeit far better off than yourself, considering your respective styles of living, persist in looking to you for assistance.

[2] See Dr. Holden ad loc., Boeckh [Bk. iii. ch. xxiii.], p. 465 f.

[3] Cf. Lycurg. "c. Leocr. " 139.

[4] Al. "presidential duties. "

[5] {trierarkhias [misthous]}. The commentators in general "suspect" {misthous}. See Boeckh, "P. E. A. " p. 579.

[6] See Boeckh, p. 470 f. ; "Revenues, " iii. 9, iv. 40.

[7] Or, "to childish matters, " "frivolous affairs"; but for the full import of the phrase {paidikois pragmasi} see "Ages. " viii. 2.

The Economist

Then Critobulus: I cannot gainsay what you have spoken, Socrates, it is indeed high time that you were constituted my patronus, or I shall become in very truth a pitiable object.

To which appeal Socrates made answer: Why, you yourself must surely be astonished at the part you are now playing. Just now, when I said that I was rich, you laughed at me as if I had no idea what riches were, and you were not happy till you had cross-examined me and forced me to confess that I do not possess the hundredth part of what you have; and now you are imploring me to be your patron, and to stint no pains to save you from becoming absolutely and in very truth a pauper. [8]

[8] Or, "literally beggared."

Crit. Yes, Socrates, for I see that you are skilled in one lucrative operation at all events—the art of creating a surplus. I hope, therefore, that a man who can make so much out of so little will not have the slightest difficulty in creating an ample surplus out of an abundance.

Soc. But do not you recollect how just now in the discussion you would hardly let me utter a syllable[9] while you laid down the law: if a man did not know how to handle horses, horses were not wealth to him at any rate; nor land, nor sheep, nor money, nor anything else, if he did not know how to use them? And yet these are the very sources of revenue from which incomes are derived; and how do you expect me to know the use of any of them who never possessed a single one of them since I was born?

[9] Cf. Aristoph. "Clouds," 945; "Plut." 17; Dem. 353; and Holden ad loc.

Crit. Yes, but we agreed that, however little a man may be blest with wealth himself, a science of economy exists; and that being so, what hinders you from being its professor?

Soc. Nothing, to be sure, [10] except what would hinder a man from knowing how to play the flute, supposing he had never had a flute of his own and no one had supplied the defect by lending him one to practise on: which is just my case with regard to economy, [11] seeing I never myself possessed the instrument of the science which is wealth, so as to go through the pupil stage, nor hitherto has any

The Economist

one proposed to hand me over his to manage. You, in fact, are the first person to make so generous an offer. You will bear in mind, I hope, that a learner of the harp is apt to break and spoil the instrument; it is therefore probable, if I take in hand to learn the art of economy on your estate, I shall ruin it outright.

[10] Lit. "The very thing, God help me! which would hinder . . . "

[11] Lit. "the art of administering an estate. "

Critobulus retorted: I see, Socrates, you are doing your very best to escape an irksome task: you would rather not, if you can help it, stretch out so much as your little finger to help me to bear my necessary burthens more easily.

Soc. No, upon my word, I am not trying to escape: on the contrary, I shall be ready, as far as I can, to expound the matter to you. [12] . .. Still it strikes me, if you had come to me for fire, and I had none in my house, you would not blame me for sending you where you might get it; or if you had asked me for water, and I, having none to give, had led you elsewhere to the object of your search, you would not, I am sure, have disapproved; or did you desire to be taught music by me, and I were to point out to you a far more skilful teacher than myself, who would perhaps be grateful to you moreover for becoming his pupil, what kind of exception could you take to my behaviour?

[12] Or, "to play the part of {exegetes}, 'legal adviser, ' or 'spiritual director, ' to be in fact your 'guide, philosopher, and friend. '"

Crit. None, with any show of justice, Socrates.

Soc. Well, then, my business now is, Critobulus, to point out[13] to you some others cleverer than myself about those matters which you are so anxious to be taught by me. I do confess to you, I have made it long my study to discover who among our fellow-citizens in this city are the greatest adepts in the various branches of knowledge. [14] I had been struck with amazement, I remember, to observe on some occasion that where a set of people are engaged in identical operations, half of them are in absolute indigence and the other half roll in wealth. I bethought me, the history of the matter was worth investigation. Accordingly I set to work investigating, and I found that it all happened very naturally. Those who carried on their affairs in a haphazard manner I saw were punished by their losses; whilst those who kept their wits upon the stretch and paid attention I soon perceived to be rewarded by the greater ease and profit of their undertakings. [15] It is to these I would recommend you to betake yourself. What say you? Learn of them: and unless the will of God oppose, [16] I venture to say you will become as clever a man of business as one might hope to see.

[13] Al. "to show you that there are others."

[14] Or, "who are gifted with the highest knowledge in their respective concerns." Cf. "Mem." IV. vii. 1.

[15] Lit. "got on quicker, easier, and more profitably."

[16] Or, "short of some divine interposition."

III

Critobulus, on hearing that, exclaimed: Be sure, Socrates, I will not let you go now until you give the proofs which, in the presence of our friends, you undertook just now to give me.

Well then, [1] Critobulus (Socrates replied), what if I begin by showing[2] you two sorts of people, the one expending large sums on money in building useless houses, the other at far less cost erecting dwellings replete with all they need; will you admit that I have laid my finger here on one of the essentials of economy?

[1] Lincke [brackets as an editorial interpolation iii. 1, {ti oun, ephe}—vi. 11, {poiomen}]. See his edition "Xenophons Dialog. {peri oikonomias} in seiner ursprunglichen Gestalt"; and for a criticism of his views, an article by Charles D. Morris, "Xenophon's Oeconomicus, " in the "American Journal of Philology, " vol. i. p. 169 foll.

[2] As a demonstrator.

Crit. An essential point most ceertainly.

Soc. And suppose in connection with the same, I next point out to you[3] two other sets of persons: —The first possessors of furniture of various kinds, which they cannot, however, lay their hands on when the need arises; indeed they hardly know if they have got all safe and sound or not: whereby they put themselves and their domestics to much mental torture. The others are perhaps less amply, or at any rate not more amply supplied, but they have everything ready at the instant for immediate use.

[3] "As in a mirror, or a picture. "

Crit. Yes, Socrates, and is not the reason simply that in the first case everything is thrown down where it chanced, whereas those others have everything arranged, each in its appointed place?

Quite right (he answered), and the phrase implies that everything is orderly arranged, not in the first chance place, but in that to which it naturally belongs.

Crit. Yes, the case is to the point, I think, and does involve another economic principle.

Soc. What, then, if I exhibit to you a third contrast, which bears on the condition of domestic slaves? On the one side you shall see them fettered hard and fast, as I may say, and yet for ever breaking their chains and running away. On the other side the slaves are loosed, and free to move, but for all that, they choose to work, it seems; they are constant to their masters. I think you will admit that I here point out another function of economy[4] worth noting.

[4] Or, "economical result."

Crit. I do indeed—a feature most noteworthy.

Soc. Or take, again, the instance of two farmers engaged in cultivating farms[5] as like as possible. The one had never done asserting that agriculture has been his ruin, and is in the depth of despair; the other has all he needs in abundance and of the best, and how acquired? —by this same agriculture.

[5] {georgias}. See Hartman, "An. Xen." p. 193. Hold. cf. Plat. "Laws," 806 E. Isocr. "Areop." 32.

Yes (Critobulus answered), to be sure; perhaps[6] the former spends both toil and money not simply on what he needs, but on things which cause an injury to house alike and owner.

[6] Or, "like enough in the one case the money and pains are spent," etc.

Soc. That is a possible case, no doubt, but it is not the one that I refer to; I mean people pretending they are farmers, and yet they have not a penny to expend on the real needs of their business.

Crit. And pray, what may be the reason of that, Socrates?

Soc. You shall come with me, and see these people also; and as you contemplate the scene, I presume you will lay to heart the lesson.

Crit. I will, if possibly I can, I promise you.

The Economist

Soc. Yes, and while you contemplate, you must make trial of yourself and see if you have wit to understand. At present, I will bear you witness that if it is to go and see a party of players performing in a comedy, you will get up at cock-crow, and come trudging a long way, and ply me volubly with reasons why I should accompany you to see the play. But you have never once invited me to come and witness such an incident as those we were speaking of just now.

Crit. And so I seem to you ridiculous? [7]

[7] Or, "a comic character in the performance. " Soc. "Not so comic as you must appear to yourself (i. e. with your keen sense of the ludicrous). "

Soc. Far more ridiculous to yourself, I warrant. But now let me point out to you another contrast: between certain people whose dealing with horses has brought them to the brink of poverty, and certain others who have found in the same pursuit the road to affluence, [8] and have a right besides to plume themselves upon their gains. [9]

[8] Or, "who have not only attained to affluence by the same pursuit, but can hold their heads high, and may well pride themselves on their thrift. "

[9] Cf. Hom. "Il. " xii. 114, {ippoisin kai okhesphin agallomenos}, et passim; "Hiero, " viii. 5; "Anab. " II. vi. 26.

Crit. Well, then, I may tell you, I see and know both characters as well as you do; but I do not find myself a whit the more included among those who gain.

Soc. Because you look at them just as you might at the actors in a tragedy or comedy, and with the same intent—your object being to delight the ear and charm the eye, but not, I take it, to become yourself a poet. And there you are right enough, no doubt, since you have no desire to become a playright. But, when circumstances compel you to concern yourself with horsemanship, does it not seem to you a little foolish not to consider how you are to escape being a mere amateur in the matter, especially as the same creatures which are good for use are profitable for sale?

Crit. So you wish me to set up as a breeder of young horses, [10] do you, Socrates?

[10] See "Horsemanship," ii. 1.

Soc. Not so, no more than I would recommend you to purchase lads and train them up from boyhood as farm-labourers. But in my opinion there is a certain happy moment of growth whuch must be seized, alike in man and horse, rich in present service and in future promise. In further illustration, I can show you how some men treat their wedded wives in such a way that they find in them true helpmates to the joint increase of their estate, while others treat them in a way to bring upon themselves wholesale disaster. [11]

[11] Reading {e os pleista}, al. {e oi pleistoi} = "to bring about disaster in most cases."

Crit. Ought the husband or the wife to bear the blame of that?

Soc. If it goes ill with the sheep we blame the shepherd, as a rule, or if a horse shows vice we throw the blame in general upon the rider. But in the case of women, supposing the wife to have received instruction from her husband and yet she delights in wrong-doing, [12] it may be that the wife is justly held to blame; but supposing he has never tried to teach her the first principles of "fair and noble" conduct, [13] and finds her quite an ignoramus[14] in these matters, surely the husband will be justly held to blame. But come now (he added), we are all friends here; make a clean breast of it, and tell us, Critobulus, the plain unvarnished truth: Is there an one to whom you are more in the habit of entrusting matters of importance than to your wife?

[12] Cf. "Horsemanship," vi. 5, of a horse "to show vice."

[13] Or, "things beautiful and of good report."

[14] Al. "has treated her as a dunce, devoid of this high knowledge."

Crit. There is no one.

Soc. And is there any one with whom you are less in the habit of conversing than with your wife?

Crit. Not many, I am forced to admit.

The Economist

Soc. And when you married her she was quite young, a mere girl—at an age when, as far as seeing and hearing go, she had the smallest acquaintance with the outer world?

Crit. Certainly.

Soc. Then would it not be more astonishing that she should have real knowledge how to speak and act than that she should go altogether astray?

Crit. But let me ask you a question, Socrates: have those happy husbands, you tell us of, who are blessed with good wives educated them themselves?

Soc. There is nothing like investigation. I will introduce you to Aspasia, [15] who will explain these matters to you in a far more scientific way than I can. My belief is that a good wife, being as she is the partner in a common estate, must needs be her husband's counterpoise and counterpart for good; since, if it is through the transactions of the husband, as a rule, that goods of all sorts find their way into the house, yet it is by means of the wife's economy and thrift that the greater part of the expenditure is checked, and on the successful issue or the mishandling of the same depends the increase or impoverishment of a whole estate. And so with regard to the remaining arts and sciences, I think I can point out to you the ablest performers in each case, if you feel you have any further need of help. [16]

[15] Aspasia. See "Mem. " II. vi. 36.

[16] Al. "there are successful performers in each who will be happy to illustrate any point in which you think you need, " etc.

IV

But why need you illustrate all the sciences, Socrates? (Critobulus asked): it would not be very easy to discover efficient craftsmen of all the arts, and quite impossible to become skilled in all one's self. So, please, confine yourself to the nobler branches of knowledge as men regard them, such as it will best befit me to pursue with devotion; be so good as to point me out these and their performers, and, above all, contribute as far as in you lies the aid of your own personal instruction.

Soc. A good suggestion, Critobulus, for the base mechanic arts, so called, have got a bad name; and what is more, are held in ill repute by civilised communities, and not unreasonably; seeing they are the ruin of the bodies of all concerned in them, workers and overseers alike, who are forced to remain in sitting postures and to hug the loom, or else to crouch whole days confronting a furnace. Hand in hand with physical enervation follows apace enfeeblement of soul: while the demand which these base mechanic arts makes on the time of those employed in them leaves them no leisure to devote to the claims of friendship and the state. How can such folk be other than sorry friends and ill defenders of the fatherland? So much so that in some states, especially those reputed to be warlike, no citizen[1] is allowed to exercise any mechanical craft at all.

[1] "In the strict sense, " e. g. the Spartiates in Sparta. See "Pol. Lac. " vii. ; Newman, op. cit. i. 99, 103 foll.

Crit. Then which are the arts you would counsel us to engage in?

Soc. Well, we shall not be ashamed, I hope, to imitate the kings of Persia? [2] That monarch, it is said, regards amongst the noblest and most necessary pursuits two in particular, which are the arts of husbandry and war, and in these two he takes the strongest interest.

[2] "It won't make us blush actually to take a leaf out of the great king's book. " As to the Greek text at this point see the commentators, and also a note by Mr. H. Richers in the "Classical Review, " x. 102.

The Economist

What! (Critobulus exclaimed); do you, Socrates, really believe that the king of Persia pays a personal regard to husbandry, along with all his other cares?

Soc. We have only to investigate the matter, Critobulus, and I daresay we shall discover whether this is so or not. We are agreed that he takes strong interest in military matters; since, however numerous the tributary nations, there is a governor to each, and every governor has orders from the king what number of cavalry, archers, slingers and targeteers[3] it is his business to support, as adequate to control the subject population, or in case of hostile attack to defend the country. Apart from these the king keeps garrisons in all the citadels. The actual support of these devolves upon the governor, to whom the duty is assigned. The king himself meanwhile conducts the annual inspection and review of troops, both mercenary and other, that have orders to be under arms. These all are simultaneously assembled (with the exception of the garrisons of citadels) at the mustering ground, [4] so named. That portion of the army within access of the royal residence the king reviews in person; the remainder, living in remoter districts of the empire, he inspects by proxy, sending certain trusty representatives. [5] Wherever the commandants of garrisons, the captains of thousands, and the satraps[6] are seen to have their appointed members complete, and at the same time shall present their troops equipped with horse and arms in thorough efficiency, these officers the king delights to honour, and showers gifts upon them largely. But as to those officers whom he finds either to have neglected their garrisons, or to have made private gain of their position, these he heavily chastises, deposing them from office, and appointing other superintendents[7] in their stead. Such conduct, I think we may say, indisputably proves the interest which he takes in matters military.

[3] Or, Gerrophoroi, "wicker-shield bearers."

[4] Or, "rendezvous"; "the 'Champ de Mars' for the nonce." Cf. "Cyrop." VI. ii. 11.

[5] Lit. "he sends some of the faithful to inspect." Cf. our "trusty and well-beloved."

[6] See, for the system, Herod. iii. 89 foll.; "Cyrop." VIII. vi. 11.

[7] Or, as we say, "inspecting officers." Cf. "Cyrop." VIII. i. 9.

The Economist

Further than this, by means of a royal progress through the country, he has an opportunity of inspecting personally some portion of his territory, and again of visiting the remainder in proxy as above by trusty representatives; and wheresoever he perceives that any of his governors can present to him a district thickly populated, and the soil in a state of active cultivation, full of trees and fruits, its natural products, to such officers he adds other territory, adorning them with gifts and distinguishing them by seats of honour. But those officers whose land he sees lying idle and with but few inhabitants, owing either to the harshness of their government, their insolence, or their neglect, he punishes, and making them to cease from their office he appoints other rulers in their place. . .. Does not this conduct indicate at least as great an anxiety to promote the active cultivation of the land by its inhabitants as to provide for its defence by military occupation? [8]

[8] Lit. "by those who guard and garrison it."

Moreover, the governors appointed to preside over these two departments of state are not one and the same. But one class governs the inhabitants proper including the workers of the soil, and collects the tribute from them, another is in command of the armed garrisons. If the commandant[9] protects the country insufficiently, the civil governor of the population, who is in charge also of the productive works, lodges accusation against the commandant to the effect that the inhabitants are prevented working through deficiency of protection. Or if again, in spite of peace being secured to the works of the land by the military governor, the civil authority still presents a territory sparse in population and untilled, it is the commandant's turn to accuse the civil ruler. For you may take it as a rule, a population tilling their territory badly will fail to support their garrisons and be quite unequal to paying their tribute. Where a satrap is appointed he has charge of both departments. [10]

[9] Or, "garrison commandant." Lit. "Phrourarch."

[10] The passage reads like a gloss. See about the Satrap, "Hell." III. i. 10; "Cyrop." VIII. vi. 1; "Anab." I. ix. 29 foll.

Thereupon Critobulus: Well, Socrates (said he), if such is his conduct, I admit that the great king does pay attention to agriculture no less than to military affairs.

And besides all this (proceeded Socrates), nowhere among the various countries which he inhabits or visits does he fail to make it his first care that there shall be orchards and gardens, parks and "paradises, " as they are called, full of all fair and noble products which the earth brings forth; and within these chiefly he spends his days, when the season of the year permits.

Crit. To be sure, Socrates, it is a natural and necessary conclusion that when the king himself spends so large a portion of his time there, his paradises should be furnished to perfection with trees and all else beautiful that earth brings forth.

Soc. And some say, Critobulus, that when the king gives gifts, he summons in the first place those who have shown themselves brave warriors, since all the ploughing in the world were but small gain in the absence of those who should protect the fields; and next to these he summons those who have stocked their countries best and rendered them productive, on the principle that but for the tillers of the soil the warriors themselves could scarcely live. And there is a tale told of Cyrus, the most famous prince, I need not tell you, who ever wore a crown, [11] how on one occasion he said to those who had been called to receive the gifts, "it were no injustice, if he himself received the gifts due to warriors and tillers of the soil alike, " for "did he not carry off the palm in stocking the country and also in protecting the goods with which it had been stocked? "

[11] Lit. "the most glorious king that ever lived. " The remark would seem to apply better to Cyrus the Great. Nitsche and others regard these SS. 18, 19 as interpolated. See Schenkl ad loc.

Crit. Which clearly shows, Socrates, if the tale be true, that this same Cyrus took as great a pride in fostering the productive energies of his country and stocking it with good things, as in his reputation as a warrior.

Soc. Why, yes indeed, had Cyrus lived, I have no doubt he would have proved the best of rulers, and in support of this belief, apart from other testimony amply furnished by his life, witness what happened when he marched to do battle for the soveriegnty of Persia with his brother. Not one man, it is said, [12] deserted from Cyrus to the king, but from the king to Cyrus tens of thousands. And this also I deem a great testimony to a ruler's worth, that his followers follow him of their own free will, and when the moment of danger comes refuse to part from him. [13] Now this was the case with Cyrus. His friends not only fought their battles side by side with him while he lived, but when he died they too died battling around his dead body, one and all, excepting only Ariaeus, who was absent at his post on the left wing of the army. [14] But there is another tale of this same Cyrus in connection with Lysander, who himself narrated it on one occasion to a friend of his in Megara. [15]

[12] Cf. "Anab. " I. ix. 29 foll.

[13] Cf. "Hiero, " xi. 12, and our author passim.

[14] See "Anab. " ib. 31.

[15] Possibly to Xenophon himself {who may have met Lysander on his way back after the events of the "Anabasis, " and implying this dialogue is concocted, since Socrates died before Xenophon returned to Athens, if he did return at that period. }

Lysander, it seems, had gone with presents sent by the Allies to Cyrus, who entertained him, and amongst other marks of courtesy showed him his "paradise" at Sardis. [16] Lysander was astonished at the beauty of the trees within, all planted[17] at equal intervals, the long straight rows of waving branches, the perfect regularity, the rectangular[18] symmetry of the whole, and the many sweet scents which hung about them as they paced the park. In admiration he exclaimed to Cyrus: "All this beauty is marvellous enough, but what astonishes me still more is the talent of the artificer who mapped out and arranged for you the several parts of this fair scene. "[19] Cyrus was pleased by the remark, and said: "Know then, Lysander, it is I who measured and arranged it all. Some of the trees, " he added, "I planted with my own hands. " Then Lysander, regarding earnestly the speaker, when he saw the beauty of his apparel and perceived its fragrance, the splendour[20] also of the necklaces and armlets, and other ornaments which he wore, exclaimed: "What say you, Cyrus? did you with your own hands plant some of these trees? " whereat the other: "Does that surprise you, Lysander? I swear to you by Mithres, [21] when in ordinary health I never dream of sitting down to supper without first practising some exercise of war or husbandry in the sweat of my brow, or venturing some strife of honour, as suits my mood. " "On hearing this, " said Lysander to his friend, "I could not help seizing him by the hand and exclaiming, 'Cyrus, you have indeed good right to be a happy man, [22] since you are happy in being a good man.'"[23]

[16] See "Hell." I. v. 1.

[17] Reading {oi' isou pephuteumena}, or if {ta pephuteumena}, transl. "the various plants ranged."

[18] Cf. Dion. Hal. "de Comp." p. 170; Cic. "de Senect." S. 59.

[19] Lit. "of these" {deiktikos}, i.e. pointing to the various beauties of the scenery.

[20] Reading {to kallos}.

[21] The Persian "Sun-God." See "Cyrop." VII. v. 53; Strab. xv. 3. 13.

[22] Or, "fortunate."

[23] Or, "you are a good man, and thereby fortunate."

V

All this I relate to you (continued Socrates) to show you that quite high and mighty[1] people find it hard to hold aloof from agrictulture, devotion to which art would seem to be thrice blest, combining as it does a certain sense of luxury with the satisfaction of an improved estate, and such a training of physical energies as shall fit a man to play a free man's part. [2] Earth, in the first place, freely offers to those that labour all things necessary to the life of man; and, as if that were not enough, makes further contribution of a thousand luxuries. [3] It is she who supplies with sweetest scent and fairest show all things wherewith to adorn the altars and statues of the gods, or deck man's person. It is to her we owe our many delicacies of flesh or fowl or vegetable growth; [4] since with the tillage of the soil is closely linked the art of breeding sheep and cattle, whereby we mortals may offer sacrifices well pleasing to the gods, and satisfy our personal needs withal.

[1] Lit. "Not even the most blessed of mankind can abstain from. " See Plat. "Rep. " 344 B, "The superlatively best and well-to-do. "

[2] Lit. "Devotion to it would seem to be at once a kind of luxury, an increase of estate, a training of the bodily parts, so that a man is able to perform all that a free man should. "

[3] Al. "and further, to the maintenance of life she adds the sources of pleasure in life. "

[4] Lit. "she bears these and rears those. "

And albeit she, good cateress, pours out her blessings upon us in abundance, yet she suffers not her gifts to be received effeminately, but inures her pensioners to suffer glady summer's heat and winter's cold. Those that labour with their hands, the actual delvers of the soil, she trains in a wrestling school of her own, adding strength to strength; whilst those others whose devotion is confined to the overseeing eye and to studious thought, she makes more manly, rousing them with cock-crow, and compelling them to be up and doing in many a long day's march. [5] Since, whether in city or afield, with the shifting seasons each necessary labour has its hour of performance. [6]

The Economist

[5] See "Hellenica Essays, " p. 341.

[6] Lit. "each most necessary operation must ever be in season. "

Or to turn to another side. Suppose it to be a man's ambition to aid his city as a trooper mounted on a charger of his own: why not combine the rearing of horses with other stock? it is the farmer's chance. [7] Or would your citizen serve on foot? It is husbandry that shall give him robustness of body. Or if we turn to the toil-loving fascination of the chase, [8] here once more earth adds incitement, as well as furnishing facility of sustenance for the dogs as by nurturing a foster brood of wild animals. And if horses and dogs derive benefit from this art of husbandry, they in turn requite the boon through service rendered to the farm. The horse carries his best of friends, the careful master, betimes to the scene of labour and devotion, and enables him to leave it late. The dog keeps off the depredations of wild animals from fruits and flocks, and creates security in the solitary place.

[7] Lit. "farming is best adapted to rearing horses along with other produce. "

[8] Lit. "to labour willingly and earnestly at hunting earth helps to incite us somewhat. "

Earth, too, adds stimulus in war-time to earth's tillers; she pricks them on to aid the country under arms, and this she does by fostering her fruits in open field, the prize of valour for the mightiest. [9] For this also is the art athletic, this of husbandry; as thereby men are fitted to run, and hurl the spear, and leap with the best. [10]

[9] Cf. "Hipparch, " viii. 8.

[10] Cf. "Hunting, " xii. 1 foll.

This, too, is that kindliest of arts which makes requital tenfold in kind for every work of the labourer. [11] She is the sweet mistress who, with smile of welcome and outstretched hand, greets the approach of her devoted one, seeming to say, Take from me all thy heart's desire. She is the generous hostess; she keeps open house for the stranger. [12] For where else, save in some happy rural seat of her devising, shall a man more cheerily cherish content in winter, with bubbling bath and blazing fire? or where, save afield, in summer rest more sweetly, lulled by babbling streams, soft airs, and tender shades? [13]

[11] Lit. "What art makes an ampler return for their labour to those who work for her? What art more sweetly welcomes him that is devoted to her?"

[12] Lit. "What art welcomes the stranger with greater prodigality?"

[13] See "Hellenica Essays," p. 380; and as still more to the point, Cowley's Essays: "Of Agriculture," passim.

Her high prerogative it is to offer fitting first-fruits to high heaven, hers to furnish forth the overflowing festal board. [14] Hers is a kindly presence in the household. She is the good wife's favourite, the children long for her, she waves her hand winningly to the master's friends.

[14] Or, "to appoint the festal board most bounteously."

For myself, I marvel greatly if it has ever fallen to the lot of freeborn man to own a choicer possesion, or to discover an occupation more seductive, or of wider usefulness in life than this.

But, furthermore, earth of her own will[15] gives lessons in justice and uprightness to all who can understand her meaning, since the nobler the service of devotion rendered, the ampler the riches of her recompense. [16] One day, perchance, these pupils of hers, whose conversation in past times was in husbandry, [17] shall, by reason of the multitude of invading armies, be ousted from their labours. The work of their hands may indeed be snatched from them, but they were brought up in stout and manly fashion. They stand, each one of them, in body and soul equipped; and, save God himself shall hinder them, they will march into the territory of those their human hinderers, and take from them the wherewithal to support their lives. Since often enough in war it is surer and safer to quest for food with sword and buckler than with all the instruments of husbandry.

[15] Reading {thelousa}, vulg., or if after Cobet, {theos ousa}, transl. "by sanction of her divinity." With {thelousa} Holden aptly compares Virgil's "volentia rura," "Georg." ii. 500.

[16] "That is, her 'lex talionis.'"

[17] "Engaged long time in husbandry."

But there is yet another lesson to be learnt in the public shool of husbandry[18]—the lesson of mutual assistance. "Shoulder to shoulder" must we march to meet the invader; [19] "shoulder to shoulder" stand to compass the tillage of the soil. Therefore it is that the husbandman, who means to win in his avocation, must see that he creates enthusiasm in his workpeople and a spirit of ready obedience; which is just what a general attacking an enemy will scheme to bring about, when he deals out gifts to the brave and castigation[20] to those who are disorderly.

[18] Lit. "But again, husbandry trains up her scholars side by side in lessons of . ..."

[19] {sun anthropois}, "man with his fellow-man, " is the "mot d'order" (cf. the author's favourite {sun theois}); "united human effort."

[20] "Lashes, " "punishment. " Cf. "Anab. " II. vi. 10, of Clearchus.

Nor will there be lacking seasons of exhortation, the general haranguing his troops and the husbandman his labourers; nor because they are slaves do they less than free men need the lure of hope and happy expectation, [21] that they may willingly stand to their posts.

[21] "The lure of happy prospects. " See "Horsmanship, " iii. 1.

It was an excellent saying of his who named husbandry "the mother and nurse of all the arts, " for while agriculture prospers all other arts like are vigorous and strong, but where the land is forced to remain desert, [22] the spring that feeds the other arts is dried up; they dwindle, I had almost said, one and all, by land and sea.

[22] Or, "lie waste and barren as the blown sea-sand. "

These utterances drew from Critobulus a comment:

Socrates (he said), for my part I agree with all you say; only, one must face the fact that in agriculture nine matters out of ten are beyond man's calculation. Since at one time hailstones and another frost, at another drought or a deluge of rain, or mildew, or other pest, will obliterate all the fair creations and designs of men; or behold, his fleecy flocks most fairly nurtured, then comes murrain, and the end most foul destruction. [23]

[23] See Virg. "Georg. " iii. 441 foll. : "Turpis oves tentat scabies, ubi frigidus imber. "

To which Socrates: Nay, I thought, Critobulus, you full surely were aware that the operations of husbandry, no less than those of war, lie in the hands of the gods. I am sure you will have noted the behaviour of men engaged in war; how on the verge of military operations they strive to win the acceptance of the divine powers; [24] how eagerly they assail the ears of heaven, and by dint of sacrifices and omens seek to discover what they should and what they should not do. So likewise as regards the processes of husbandry, think you the propitiation of heaven is less needed here? Be well assured (he added) the wise and prudent will pay service to the gods on behalf of moist fruits and dry, [25] on behalf of cattle and horses, sheep and goats; nay, on behalf of all their possessions, great and small, without exception.

[24] See "Hell. " III. i. 16 foll., of Dercylidas.

[25] "Every kind of produce, succulent (like the grape and olive) or dry (like wheat and barley, etc.)"

The Economist

VI

Your words (Critobulus answered) command my entire sympathy, when you bid us endeavour to begin each work with heaven's help, [1] seeing that the gods hold in their hands the issues alike of peace and war. So at any rate will we endeavour to act at all times; but will you now endeavour on your side to continue the discussion of economy from the point at which you broke off, and bring it point by point to its conclusion? What you have said so far has not been thrown away on me. I seem to discern already more clearly, what sort of behaviour is necessary to anything like real living. [2]

[1] Lit. "with the gods, " and for the sentiment see below, x. 10; "Cyrop. " III. i. 15; "Hipparch, " ix. 3.

[2] For {bioteuein} cf. Pind. "Nem. " iv. 11, and see Holden ad loc.

Socrates replied: What say you then? Shall we first survey the ground already traversed, and retrace the steps on which we were agreed, so that, if possible we may conduct the remaining portion of the argument to its issue with like unanimity? [3]

[3] Lit. "try whether we can go through the remaining steps with like ..."

Crit. Why, yes! If it is agreeable for two partners in a business to run through their accounts without dispute, so now as partners in an argument it will be no less agreeable to sum up the points under discussion, as you say, with unanimity.

Soc. Well, then, we agreed that economy was the proper title of a branch of knowledge, and this branch of knowledge appeared to be that whereby men are enabled to enhance the value of their houses or estates; and by this word "house or estate" we understood the whole of a man's possessions; and "possessions" again we defined to include those things which the possessor should find advantageous for the purposes of his life; and things advantageous finally were discovered to mean all that a man knows how to use and turn to good account. Further, for a man to learn all branches of knowledge not only seemed to us an impossibility, but we thought we might well follow the example of civil communties in rejecting the base mechanic arts so called, on the ground that they destroy the bodies of the artisans, as far as we can see, and crush their spirits.

The clearest proof of this, we said, [4] could be discovered if, on the occasion of a hostile inroad, one were to seat the husbandmen and the artisans apart in two divisions, and then proceed to put this question to each group in turn: "Do you think it better to defend our country districts or to retire from the fields[5] and guard the walls? " And we anticipated that those concerned with the soil would vote to defend the soil; while the artisans would vote not to fight, but, in docile obedience to their training, to sit with folded hands, neither expending toil nor venturing their lives.

[4] This S. 6 has no parallel supra. See Breit. and Schenkl ad loc. for attempts to cure the text.

[5] See Cobet, "N. L." 580, reading {uphemenous}, or if {aphemenous} transl. "to abandon. "

Next we held it as proved that there was no better employment for a gentleman—we described him as a man beautiful and good—than this of husbandry, by which human beings procure to themselves the necessaries of life. This same employment, moreover, was, as we agreed, at once the easiest to learn[6] and the pleasantest to follow, since it gives to the limbs beauty and hardihood, whilst permitting[7] to the soul leisure to satisfy the claims of friendship and of civic duty.

[6] {raste mathein}. Vide infra, not supra.

[7] Lit. "least allowing the soul no leisure to care for friends and state withal. "

Again it seemed to us that husbandry acts as a spur to bravery in the hearts of those that till the fields, [8] inasmuch as the necessaries of life, vegetable and animal, under her auspices spring up and are reared outside the fortified defences of the city. For which reason also this way of life stood in the highest repute in the eyes of statesmen and commonwealths, as furnishing the best citizens and those best disposed to the common weal. [9]

[8] Cf. Aristot. "Oec. " I. ii. 1343 B, {pros toutois k. t.l. }
[9] Cf. Aristoph. "Archarnians. "

Crit. I think I am fully persuaded as to the propriety of making agriculture the basis of life. I see it is altogether noblest, best, and pleasantest to do so. But I should like to revert to your remark that you understood the reason why the tillage of one man brings him in an abundance of all he needs, while the operations of another fail to make husbandry a profitable employment. I would gladly hear from you an explanation of both these points, so that I may adopt the right and avoid the harmful course. [10]

[10] Lincke conceives the editor's interpolation as ending here.

Soc. Well, Critobulus, suppose I narrate to you from the beginning how I cam in contact with a man who of all men I ever met seemed to me to deserve the appellation of a gentleman. He was indeed a "beautiful and good" man. [11]

[11] Or, "a man 'beautiful and good, ' as the phrase goes. "

Crit. There is nothing I should better like to hear, since of all titles this is the one I covet most the right to bear.

Soc. Well, then, I will tell you how I came to subject him to my inquiry. It did not take me long to go the round of various good carpenters, good bronze-workers, painters, sculptors, and so forth. A brief period was sufficient for the contemplation of themselves and of their most admired works of art. But when it came to examining those who bore the high-sounding title "beautiful and good, " in order to find out what conduct on their part justified their adoption of this title, I found my soul eager with desire for intercourse with one of them; and first of all, seeing that the epithet "beautiful" was conjoined with that of "good, " every beautiful person I saw, I must needs approach in my endeavour to discover, [12] if haply I might somewhere see the quality of good adhering to the quality of beauty. But, after all, it was otherwise ordained. I soon enough seemed to discover[13] that some of those who in their outward form were beautiful were in their inmost selves the veriest knaves. Accordingly I made up my mind to let go beauty which appeals to the eye, and address myself to one of those "beautiful and good" people so entitled. And since I heard of Ischomachus[14] as one who was so called by all the world, both men and women, strangers and citizens alike, I set myself to make acquaintance with him.

[12] Or, "and try to understand."

[13] Or, "understand."

[14] See Cobet, "Pros. Xen." s. n.

The Economist

VII

It chanced, one day I saw him seated in the portico of Zeus Eleutherios, [1] and as he appeared to be at leisure, I went up to him and, sitting down by his side, accosted him: How is this, Ischomachus? you seated here, you who are so little wont to be at leisure? As a rule, when I see you, you are doing something, or at any rate not sitting idle in the market-place.

[1] "The god of freedom, or of freed men. " See Plat. "Theag. " 259 A. The scholiast on Aristoph. "Plutus" 1176 identifies the god with Zeus Soter. See Plut. "Dem. " 859 (Clough, v. 30).

Nor would you see me now so sitting, Socrates (he answered), but that I promised to meet some strangers, friends of mine, [2] at this place.

[2] "Foreign friends. "

And when you have no such business on hand (I said) where in heaven's name do you spend your time and how do you employ yourself? I will not conceal from you how anxious I am to learn from your lips by what conduct you have earned for yourself the title "beautiful and good. "[3] It is not by spending your days indoors at home, I am sure; the whole habit of your body bears witness to a different sort of life.

[3] "The sobriquet of 'honest gentleman. '"

Then Ischomachus, smiling at my question, but also, as it seemed to me, a little pleased to be asked what he had done to earn the title "beautiful and good, " made answer: Whether that is the title by which folk call me when they talk to you about me, I cannot say; all I know is, when they challenge me to exchange properties, [4] or else to perform some service to the state instead of them, the fitting out of a trireme, or the training of a chorus, nobody thinks of asking for the beautiful and good gentleman, but it is plain Ischomachus, the son of So-and-so, [5] on whom the summons is served. But to answer your question, Socrates (he proceeded), I certainly do not spend my days indoors, if for no other reason, because my wife is quite capable of managing our domestic affairs without my aid.

[4] On the antidosis or compulsory exchange of property, see Boeckh, p. 580, Engl. ed. : "In case any man, upon whom a {leitourgia} was imposed, considered that another was richer than himself, and therefore most justly chargeable with the burden, he might challenge the other to assume the burden, or to make with him an {antidosis} or exchange of property. Such a challenge, if declined, was converted into a lawsuit, or came before a heliastic court for trial. " Gow, "Companion, " xviii. "Athenian Finance. " See Dem. "Against Midias, " 565, Kennedy, p. 117, and Appendix II. For the various liturgies, Trierarchy, Choregy, etc., see "Pol. Ath. " i. 13 foll.

[5] Or, "the son of his father, " it being customary at Athens to add the patronymic, e.g. Xenophon son of Gryllus, Thucydides son of Olorus, etc. See Herod. vi. 14, viii. 90. In official acts the name of the deme was added, eg. Demosthenes son of Demosthenes of Paiane; or of the tribe, at times. Cf. Thuc. viii. 69; Plat. "Laws, " vi. p. 753 B.

Ah! (said I), Ischomachus, that is just what I should like particularly to learn from you. Did you yourself educate your wife to be all that a wife should be, or when you received her from her father and mother was she already a proficient well skilled to discharge the duties appropriate to a wife?

Well skilled! (he replied). What proficiency was she likely to bring with her, when she was not quite fifteen[6] at the time she wedded me, and during the whole prior period of her life had been most carefully brought up[7] to see and hear as little as possible, and to ask[8] the fewest questions? or do you not think one should be satisfied, if at marriage her whole experience consisted in knowing how to take the wool and make a dress, and seeing how her mother's handmaidens had their daily spinning-tasks assigned them? For (he added), as regards control of appetite and self-indulgence, [9] she had received the soundest education, and that I take to be the most important matter in the bringing-up of man or woman.

[6] See Aristot. "Pol. " vii. 16. 1335(a). See Newman, op. cit. i. 170 foll.

[7] Or, "surveillance. " See "Pol. Lac. " i. 3.

[8] Reading {eroito}; or if with Sauppe after Cobet, {eroin}, transl. "talk as little as possible. "

[9] Al. "in reference to culinary matters. " See Mahaffy, "Social Life in Greece, " p. 276.

Then all else (said I) you taught your wife yourself, Ischomachus, until you had made her capable of attending carefully to her appointed duties?

That did I not (replied he) until I had offered sacrifice, and prayed that I might teach and she might learn all that could conduce to the happiness of us twain.

Soc. And did your wife join in sacrifice and prayer to that effect?

Isch. Most certainly, with many a vow registered to heaven to become all she ought to be; and her whole manner showed that she would not be neglectful of what was taught her. [10]

[10] Or, "giving plain proof that, if the teaching failed, it should not be from want of due attention on her part. " See "Hellenica Essays, " "Xenophon, " p. 356 foll.

Soc. Pray narrate to me, Ischomachus, I beg of you, what you first essayed to teach her. To hear that story would please me more than any description of the most splendid gymnastic contest or horse-race you could give me.

Why, Socrates (he answered), when after a time she had become accustomed to my hand, that is, was tamed[11] sufficiently to play her part in a discussion, I put to her this question: "Did it ever strike you to consider, dear wife, [12] what led me to choose you as my wife among all women, and your parents to entrust you to me of all men? It was certainly not from any difficulty that might beset either of us to find another bedfellow. That I am sure is evident to you. No! it was with deliberate intent to discover, I for myself and your parents in behalf of you, the best partner of house and children we could find, that I sought you out, and your parents, acting to the best of their ability, made choice of me. If at some future time God grant us to have children born to us, we will take counsel together how best to bring them up, for that too will be a common interest, [13] and a common blessing if haply they shall live to fight our battles and we find in them hereafter support and succour when ourselves are old. [14] But at present there is our house here, which belongs like to both. It is common property, for all that I possess goes by my will into the common fund, and in the same way all that you deposited[15] was placed by you to the common fund. [16] We need not stop to calculate in figures which of us contributed most, but rather let us lay to heart this fact that whichever of us proves the better partner, he or she at once contributes what is most worth having."

[11] (The timid, fawn-like creature.) See Lecky, "Hist. of Eur. Morals," ii. 305. For the metaphor cf. Dem. "Olynth." iii. 37. 9.

[12] Lit. "woman." Cf. N. T. {gunai}, St. John ii. 4; xix. 26.

[13] Or, "our interests will centre in them; it will be a blessing we share in common to train them that they shall fight our battles, and . .."

[14] Cf. "Mem." II. ii. 13. Holden cf. Soph. "Ajax." 567; Eur. "Suppl." 918.

[15] Or reading {epenegke} with Cobet, "brought with you in the way of dowry."

[16] Or, "to the joint estate."

Thus I addressed her, Socrates, and thus my wife made answer: "But how can I assist you? what is my ability? Nay, everything depends on you. My business, my mother told me, was to be sober-minded!"[17]

[17] "Modest and temperate," and (below) "temperance."

"Most true, my wife," I replied, "and that is what my father said to me. But what is the proof of sober-mindedness in man or woman? Is it not so to behave that what they have of good may ever be at its best, and that new treasures from the same source of beauty and righteousness may be most amply added?"

"But what is there that I can do," my wife inquired, "which will help to increase our joint estate?"

"Assuredly," I answered, "you may strive to do as well as possible what Heaven has given you a natural gift for and which the law approves."

The Economist

"And what may these things be? " she asked.

"To my mind they are not the things of least importance, " I replied, "unless the things which the queen bee in her hive presides over are of slight importance to the bee community; for the gods" (so Ischomachus assured me, he continued), "the gods, my wife, would seem to have exercised much care and judgment in compacting that twin system which goes by the name of male and female, so as to secure the greatest possible advantage[18] to the pair. Since no doubt the underlying principle of the bond is first and foremost to perpetuate through procreation the races of living creatures; [19] and next, as the outcome of this bond, for human beings at any rate, a provision is made by which they may have sons and daughters to support them in old age.

[18] Reading {oti}, or if with Br. {eti . .. auto}, "with the further intent it should prove of maximum advantage to itself. "

[19] Cf. (Aristot.) "Oecon. " i. 3.

"And again, the way of life of human beings, not being maintained like that of cattle[20] in the open air, obviously demands roofed homesteads. But if these same human beings are to have anything to bring in under cover, some one to carry out these labours of the field under high heaven[21] must be found them, since such operations as the breaking up of fallow with the plough, the sowing of seed, the planting of trees, the pasturing and herding of flocks, are one and all open-air employments on which the supply of products necessary to life depends.

[20] "And the beast of the field. "

[21] "Sub dis, " "in the open air. "

"As soon as these products of the field are safely housed and under cover, new needs arise. There must be some one to guard the store and some one to perform such necessary operations as imply the need of shelter. [22] Shelter, for instance, is needed for the rearing of infant children; shelter is needed for the various processes of converting the fruits of earth into food, and in like manner for the fabrication of clothing out of wool.

[22] Or, "works which call for shelter. "

"But whereas both of these, the indoor and the outdoor occupations alike, demand new toil and new attention, to meet the case, " I added, "God made provision[23] from the first by shaping, as it seems to me, the woman's nature for indoor and the man's for outdoor occupations. Man's body and soul He furnished with a greater capacity for enduring heat and cold, wayfaring and military marches; or, to repeat, He laid upon his shoulders the outdoor works.

[23] "Straightway from the moment of birth provided. " Cf. (Aristot.) "Oecon. " i. 3, a work based upon or at any rate following the lines of Xenophon's treatise.

"While in creating the body of woman with less capacity for these things, " I continued, "God would seem to have imposed on her the indoor works; and knowing that He had implanted in the woman and imposed upon her the nurture of new-born babies, He endowed her with a larger share of affection for the new-born child than He bestowed upon man. [24] And since He imposed on woman the guardianship of the things imported from without, God, in His wisdom, perceiving that a fearful spirit was no detriment to guardianship, [25] endowed the woman with a larger measure of timidity than He bestowed on man. Knowing further that he to whom the outdoor works belonged would need to defend them against malign attack, He endowed the man in turn with a larger share of courage.

[24] {edasato}, "Cyrop. " IV. ii. 43.

[25] Cf. "Hipparch, " vii. 7; Aristot. "Pol. " iii. 2; "Oecon. " iii.

"And seeing that both alike feel the need of giving and receiving, He set down memory and carefulness between them for their common use, [26] so that you would find it hard to determine which of the two, the male or the female, has the larger share of these. So, too, God set down between them for their common use the gift of self-control, where needed, adding only to that one of the twain, whether man or woman, which should prove the better, the power to be rewarded with a larger share of this perfection. And for the very reason that their natures are not alike adapted to like ends, they stand in greater need of one another; and the married couple is made more useful to itself, the one fulfilling what the other lacks. [27]

[26] Or, "He bestowed memory and carefulness as the common heritage of both. "

[27] Or, "the pair discovers the advantage of duality; the one being strong wherein the other is defective. "

"Now, being well aware of this, my wife, " I added, "and knowing well what things are laid upon us twain by God Himself, must we not strive to perform, each in the best way possible, our respective duties? Law, too, gives her consent—law and the usage of mankind, by sanctioning the wedlock of man and wife; and just as God ordained them to be partners in their children, so the law establishes their common ownership of house and estate. Custom, moreover, proclaims as beautiful those excellences of man and woman with which God gifted them at birth. [28] Thus for a woman to bide tranquilly at home rather than roam aborad is no dishonour; but for a man to remain indoors, instead of devoting himself to outdoor pursuits, is a thing discreditable. But if a man does things contrary to the nature given him by God, the chances are, [29] such insubordination escapes not the eye of Heaven: he pays the penalty, whether of neglecting his own works, or of performing those appropriate to woman. "[30]

[28] Or, "with approving fingers stamps as noble those diverse faculties, those superiorities in either sex which God created in them. Thus for the womean to remain indoors is nobler than to gad about abroad. " {ta kala . .. ; kallion . .. aiskhion . .. }— These words, wich their significant Hellenic connotation, suffer cruelly in translation.

[29] Or, "maybe in some respect this violation of the order of things, this lack of discpline on his part. " Cf. "Cyrop. " VII. ii. 6.

[30] Or, "the works of his wife. " For the sentiment cf. Soph. "Oed. Col. " 337 foll. ; Herod. ii. 35.

I added: "Just such works, if I mistake not, that same queen-bee we spoke of labours hard to perform, like yours, my wife, enjoined upon her by God Himself. "

"And what sort of works are these? " she asked; "what has the queen-bee to do that she seems so like myself, or I like her in what I have to do? "

"Why, " I answered, "she too stays in the hive and suffers not the other bees to idle. Those whose duty it is to work outside she sends forth to their labours; and all that each of them brings in, she notes and receives and stores against the day of need; but when the season for use has come, she distributes a just share to each. Again, it is she who presides over the fabric of choicely-woven cells within. She looks to it that warp and woof are wrought with speed and beauty. Under her guardian eye the brood of young[31] is nursed and reared; but when the days of rearing are past and the young bees are ripe for work, she sends them out as colonists with one of the seed royal[32] to be their leader. "

[31] Or, "the growing progeny is reared to maturity. "

[32] Or, "royal lineage, " reading {ton epigonon} (emend. H. Estienne); or if the vulg. {ton epomenon}, "with some leader of the host" (lit. of his followers). So Breitenbach.

"Shall I then have to do these things? " asked my wife.

"Yes, " I answered, "you will need in the same way to stay indoors, despatching to their toils without those of your domestics whose work lies there. Over those whose appointed tasks are wrought indoors, it will be your duty to preside; yours to receive the stuffs brought in; yours to apportion part for daily use, and yours to make provision for the rest, to guard and garner it so that the outgoings destined for a year may not be expended in a month. It will be your duty, when the wools are introduced, to see that clothing is made for those who need; your duty also to see that the dried corn is rendered fit and serviceable for food.

"There is just one of all these occupations which devolve upon you, " I added, "you may not find so altogether pleasing. Should any one of our household fall sick, it will be your care to see and tend them to the recovery of their health. "

"Nay, " she answered, "that will be my pleasantest of tasks, if careful nursing may touch the springs of gratitude and leave them friendlier than before. "

And I (continued Ischomachus) was struck with admiration at her answer, and replied: "Think you, my wife, it is through some such traits of forethought seen in their mistress-leader that the hearts of bees are won, and they are so loyally affectioned towards her that, if ever she abandon her hive, not one of them will dream of being left behind; [33] but one and all must follow her. "

[33] Al. "will suffer her to be forsaken. "

And my wife made answer to me: "It would much astonish me (said she) did not these leader's works, you speak of, point to you rather than myself. Methinks mine would be a pretty[34] guardianship and distribution of things indoors without your provident care to see that the importations from without were duly made. "

[34] Or, "ridiculous. "

"Just so, " I answered, "and mine would be a pretty[35] importation if there were no one to guard what I imported. Do you not see, " I added, "how pitiful is the case of those unfortunates who pour water in their sieves for ever, as the story goes, [36] and labour but in vain? "

[35] "As laughable an importation. "

[36] Or, "how pitiful their case, condemned, as the saying goes, to pour water into a sieve. " Lit. "filling a bucket bored with holes. " Cf. Aristot. "Oec. " i. 6; and for the Danaids, see Ovid. "Met. " iv. 462; Hor. "Carm. " iii. 11. 25; Lucr. iii. 937; Plaut. "Pseud. " 369. Cp. Coleridge:

Work without hope draws nectar in a sieve, And hope without an object cannot live.

"Pitiful enough, poor souls, " she answered, "if that is what they do. "

"But there are other cares, you know, and occupations, " I answered, "which are yours by right, and these you will find agreeable. This, for instance, to take some maiden who knows naught of carding wool and to make her proficient in the art, doubling her usefulness; or to receive another quite ignorant of housekeeping or of service, and to render her skilful, loyal, serviceable, till she is worth her weight in gold; or again, when occasion serves, you have it in your power to requite by kindness the well-behaved whose presence is a blessing to your house; or maybe to chasten the bad character, should such an one appear. But the greatest joy of all will be to prove yourself my better; to make me your faithful follower; knowing no dread lest as the years advance you should decline in honour in your household, but rather trusting that, though your hair turn gray, yet, in proportion as you come to be a better helpmate to myself and to the children, a better guardian of our home, so will your honour increase throughout the household as mistress, wife, and mother, daily more dearly prized. Since, " I added, "it is not through excellence of outward form, [37] but by reason of the lustre of virtues shed forth upon the life of man, that increase is given to things beautiful and good. "[38]

[37] "By reason of the flower on the damask cheek. "

[38] Al. "For growth is added to things 'beautiful and good, ' not through the bloom of youth but virtuous perfections, an increase coextensive with the life of man. " See Breit. ad loc.

That, Socrates, or something like that, as far as I may trust my memory, records the earliest conversation which I held with her.

VIII

And did you happen to observe, Ischomachus (I asked), whether, as the result of what was said, your wife was stirred at all to greater carefulness?

Yes, certainly (Ischomachus answered), and I remember how piqued she was at one time and how deeply she blushed, when I chanced to ask her for something which had been brought into the house, and she could not give it me. So I, when I saw her annoyance, fell to consoling her. "Do not be at all disheartened, my wife, that you cannot give me what I ask for. It is plain poverty, [1] no doubt, to need a thing and not to have the use of it. But as wants go, to look for something which I cannot lay my hands upon is a less painful form of indigence than never to dream of looking because I know full well that the thing exists not. Anyhow, you are not to blame for this, " I added; "mine the fault was who handed over to your care the things without assigning them their places. Had I done so, you would have known not only where to put but where to find them. [2] After all, my wife, there is nothing in human life so serviceable, nought so beautiful as order. [3]

[1] "Vetus proverbium, " Cic. ap. Columellam, xii. 2, 3; Nobbe, 236, fr. 6.

[2] Lit. "so that you might know not only where to put, " etc.

[3] Or, "order and arrangement. " So Cic. ap. Col. xii. 2, 4, "dispositione atque ordine. "

"For instance, what is a chorus? —a band composed of human beings, who dance and sing; but suppose the company proceed to act as each may chance—confusion follows; the spectacle has lost its charm. How different when each and all together act and recite[4] with orderly precision, the limbs and voices keeping time and tune. Then, indeed, these same performers are worth seeing and worth hearing.

[4] Or, "declaim, " {phtheggontai}, properly of the "recitative" of the chorus. Cf. Plat. "Phaedr. " 238 D.

"So, too, an army, " I said, "my wife, an army destitute of order is confusion worse confounded: to enemies an easy prey, courting attack; to friends a bitter spectacle of wasted power; [5] a mingled mob of asses, heavy infantry, and baggage-bearers, light infantry, cavalry, and waggons. Now, suppose they are on the march; how are they to get along? In this condition everybody will be a hindrance to everybody: 'slow march' side by side with 'double quick, ' 'quick march' at cross purposes with 'stand at ease'; waggons blocking cavalry and asses fouling waggons; baggage-bearers and hoplites jostling together: the whole a hopeless jumble. And when it comes to fighting, such an army is not precisely in condition to deliver battle. The troops who are compelled to retreat before the enemy's advance[6] are fully capable of trampling down the heavy infantry detachments in reserve. [7]

[5] Reading {agleukestaton}, or, if with Breit, {akleestaton}, "a most inglorious spectacle of extreme unprofitableness. "

[6] Or, "whose duty (or necessity) it is to retire before an attack, " i. e. the skirmishers. Al. "those who have to retreat, " i. e. the non-combatants.

[7] Al. "are quite capable of trampling down the troops behind in their retreat. " {tous opla ekhontas} = "the troops proper, " "heavy infantry. "

"How different is an army well organised in battle order: a splendid sight for friendly eyes to gaze at, albeit an eyesore to the enemy. For who, being of their party, but will feel a thrill of satisfaction as he watches the serried masses of heavy infantry moving onwards in unbroken order? who but will gaze with wonderment as the squadrons of the cavalry dash past him at the gallop? And what of the foeman? will not his heart sink within him to see the orderly arrangements of the different arms: [8] here heavy infantry and cavalry, and there again light infantry, there archers and there slingers, following each their leaders, with orderly precision. As they tramp onwards thus in order, though they number many myriads, yet even so they move on and on in quiet progress, stepping like one man, and the place just vacated in front is filled up on the instant from the rear.

[8] "Different styles of troops drawn up in separate divisions: hoplites, cavalry, and peltasts, archers, and slingers. "

The Economist

"Or picture a trireme, crammed choke-full of mariners; for what reason is she so terror-striking an object to her enemies, and a sight so gladsome to the eyes of friends? is it not that the gallant ship sails so swiftly? And why is it that, for all their crowding, the ship's company[9] cause each other no distress? Simply that there, as you may see them, they sit in order; in order bend to the oar; in order recover the stroke; in order step on board; in order disembark. But disorder is, it seems to me, precisely as though a man who is a husbandman should stow away[10] together in one place wheat and barley and pulse, and by and by when he has need of barley meal, or wheaten flour, or some condiment of pulse, [11] then he must pick and choose instead of laying his hand on each thing separately sorted for use.

[9] See Thuc. iii. 77. 2.

[10] "Should shoot into one place."

[11] "Vegetable stock," "kitchen." See Holden ad loc., and Prof. Mahaffy, "Old Greek Life," p. 31.

"And so with you too, my wife, if you would avoid this confusion, if you would fain know how to administer our goods, so as to lay your finger readily on this or that as you may need, or if I ask you for anything, graciously to give it me: let us, I say, select and assign[12] the appropriate place for each set of things. This shall be the place where we will put the things; and we will instruct the housekeeper that she is to take them out thence, and mind to put them back again there; and in this way we shall know whether they are safe or not. If anything is gone, the gaping space will cry out as if it asked for something back. [13] The mere look and aspect of things will argue what wants mending; [14] and the fact of knowing where each thing is will be like having it put into one's hand at once to use without further trouble or debate."

[12] {dokimasometha}, "we will write over each in turn, as it were, 'examined and approved.'"

[13] Lit. "will miss the thing that is not."

[14] "Detect what needs attention."

The Economist

I must tell you, Socrates, what strikes me as the finest and most accurate arrangement of goods and furniture it was ever my fortune to set eyes on; when I went as a sightseer on board the great Phoenician merchantman, [15] and beheld an endless quantity of goods and gear of all sorts, all separately packed and stowed away within the smallest compass. [16] I need scarce remind you (he said, continuing his narrative) what a vast amount of wooden spars and cables[17] a ship depends on in order to get to moorings; or again, in putting out to sea; [18] you know the host of sails and cordage, rigging[19] as they call it, she requires for sailing; the quantity of engines and machinery of all sorts she is armed with in case she should encounter any hostile craft; the infinitude of arms she carries, with her crew of fighting men aboard. Then all the vessels and utensils, such as people use at home on land, required for the different messes, form a portion of the freight; and besides all this, the hold is heavy laden with a mass of merchandise, the cargo proper, which the master carries with him for the sake of traffic.

[15] See Lucian, lxvi. "The Ship, " ad in. (translated by S. T. Irwin).

[16] Lit. "in the tiniest receptacle. "

[17] See Holden ad loc. re {xelina, plekta, kremasta}.

[18] "In weighing anchor. "

[19] "Suspended tackle" (as opposed to wooden spars and masts, etc.)

Well, all these different things that I have named lay packed there in a space but little larger than a fair-sized dining-room. [20] The several sorts, moreover, as I noticed, lay so well arranged, there could be no entanglement of one with other, nor were searchers needed; [21] and if all were snugly stowed, all were alike get-at- able, [22] much to the avoidance of delay if anything were wanted on the instant.

[20] Lit. "a symmetrically-shaped dining-room, made to hold ten couches. "

[21] Lit. "a searcher"; "an inquisitor. " Cf. Shakesp. "Rom. and Jul. " V. ii. 8.

[22] Lit. "not the reverse of easy to unpack, so as to cause a waste of time and waiting. "

Then the pilot's mate[23]—"the look-out man at the prow, " to give him his proper title—was, I found, so well acquainted with the place for everything that, even off the ship, [24] he could tell you where each set of things was laid and how many there were of each, just as well as any one who knows his alphabet[25] could tell you how many letters there are in Socrates and the order in which they stand.

[23] Cf. "Pol. Ath. " i. 1; Aristoph. "Knights, " 543 foll.

[24] Or, "with his eyes shut, at a distance he could say exactly. "

[25] Or, "how to spell. " See "Mem. " IV. iv. 7; Plat. "Alc. " i. 113 A.

I saw this same man (continued Ischomachus) examining at leisure[26] everything which could possibly[27] be needful for the service of the ship. His inspection caused me such surprise, I asked him what he was doing, whereupon he answered, "I am inspecting, stranger, "[28] "just considering, " says he, "the way the things are lying aboard the ship; in case of accidents, you know, to see if anything is missing, or not lying snug and shipshape. [29] There is no time left, you know, " he added, "when God mkes a tempest in the great deep, to set about searching for what you want, or to be giving out anything which is not snug and shipshape in its place. God threatens and chastises sluggards. [30] If only He destroy not innocent with guilty, a man may be content; [31] or if He turn and save all hands aboard that render right good service, [32] thanks be to Heaven. "[33]

[26] "Apparently when he had nothing better to do"; "by way of amusement. "

[27] {ara}, "as if he were asking himself, 'Would this or this possibly be wanted for the ship's service? '"

[28] "Sir. "

[29] Or, "things not lying handy in their places. "

[30] Or, "them that are slack. " Cf. "Anab. " V. viii. 15; "Mem. " IV. ii. 40; Plat. "Gorg. " 488 A: "The dolt and good-for-nothing. "

[31] "One must not grumble. "

[32] "The whole ship's crew right nobly serving. " {uperetein} = "to serve at the oar" (metaphorically = to do service to heaven).

[33] Lit. "great thanks be to the gods. "

So spoke the pilot's mate; and I, with this carefulness of stowage still before my eyes, proceeded to enforce my thesis:

"Stupid in all conscience would it be on our parts, my wife, if those who sail the sea in ships, that are but small things, can discover space and place for everything; can, moreover, in spite of violent tossings up and down, keep order, and, even while their hearts are failing them for fear, find everything they need to hand; whilst we, with all our ample storerooms[34] diversely disposed for divers objects in our mansion, an edifice firmly based[35] on solid ground, fail to discover fair and fitting places, easy of access for our several goods! Would not that argue great lack of understanding in our two selves? Well then! how good a thing it is to have a fixed and orderly arrangement of all furniture and gear; how easy also in a dwelling-house to find a place for every sort of goods, in which to stow them as shall suit each best—needs no further comment. Rather let me harp upon the string of beauty—image a fair scene: the boots and shoes and sandals, and so forth, all laid in order row upon row; the cloaks, the mantles, and the rest of the apparel stowed in their own places; the coverlets and bedding; the copper cauldrons; and all the articles for table use! Nay, though it well may raise a smile of ridicule (not on the lips of a grave man perhaps, but of some facetious witling) to hear me say it, a beauty like the cadence of sweet music[36] dwells even in pots and pans set out in neat array: and so, in general, fair things ever show more fair when orderly bestowed. The separate atoms shape themselves to form a choir, and all the space between gains beauty by their banishment. Even so some sacred chorus, [37] dancing a roundelay in honour of Dionysus, not only is a thing of beauty in itself, but the whole interspace swept clean of dancers owns a separate charm. [38]

[34] Or, "coffers, " "cupboards, " "safes. "

[35] Cf. "Anab. " III. ii. 19, "firmly planted on terra firma. "

[36] Or, "like the rhythm of a song, " {euruthmon}. See Mr. Ruskin's most appropriate note ("Bib. Past. " i. 59), "A remarkable word, as significant of the complete rhythm ({ruthmos}) whether of sound or motion, that was so great a characteristic of the Greek ideal (cf. xi. 16, {metarruthmizo}), " and much more equally to the point.

[37] "Just as a chorus, the while its dancers weave a circling dance. "

[38] Or, "contrasting with the movement and the mazes of the dance, a void appears serene and beautiful. "

"The truth of what I say, we easily can test, my wife, " I added, "by direct experiment, and that too without cost at all or even serious trouble. [39] Nor need you now distress yourself, my wife, to think how hard it will be to discover some one who has wit enough to learn the places for the several things and memory to take and place them there. We know, I fancy, that the goods of various sorts contained in the whole city far outnumber ours many thousand times; and yet you have only to bid any one of your domestics go buy this, or that, and bring it you from market, and not one of them will hesitate. The whole world knows both where to go and where to find each thing.

[39] Lit. "now whether these things I say are true (i. e. are facts), we can make experiment of the things themselves (i. e. of actual facts to prove to us). "

"And why is this? " I asked. "Merely because they lie in an appointed place. But now, if you are seeking for a human being, and that too at times when he is seeking you on his side also, often and often shall you give up the search in sheer despair: and of this again the reason? Nothing else save that no appointed place was fixed where one was to await the other. " Such, so far as I can now recall it, was the conversation which we held together touching the arrangement of our various chattels and their uses.

The Economist

IX

Well (I replied), and did your wife appear, Ischomachus, to lend a willing ear to what you tried thus earnestly to teach her?

Isch. Most certainly she did, with promise to pay all attention. Her delight was evident, like some one's who at length has found a pathway out of difficulties; in proof of which she begged me to lose no time in making the orderly arrangement I had spoken of.

And how did you introduce the order she demanded, Ischomachus? (I asked).

Isch. Well, first of all I thought I ought to show her the capacities of our house. Since you must know, it is not decked with ornaments and fretted ceilings, [1] Socrates; but the rooms were built expressly with a view to forming the most apt receptacles for whatever was intended to be put in them, so that the very look of them proclaimed what suited each particular chamber best. Thus our own bedroom, [2] secure in its position like a stronghold, claimed possession of our choicest carpets, coverlets, and other furniture. Thus, too, the warm dry rooms would seem to ask for our stock of bread-stuffs; the chill cellar for our wine; the bright and well-lit chambers for whatever works or furniture required light, and so forth.

[1] Or, "curious workmanship and paintings. " See "Mem. " III. viii. 10. Cf. Plat. "Rep. " vii. 529 B; "Hipp. maj. " 298 A. See Becker, "Charicles, " Exc. i. 111.

[2] Or, "the bridal chamber. " See Becker, op. cit. p. 266. Al. "our store-chamber. " See Hom. "Od. " xxi. 9:

{be d' imenai thalamonde sun amphipoloisi gunaixin eskhaton, k.t. l.}

"And she (Penelope) betook her, with her handmaidens, to the treasure-chamber in the uttermost part of the house, where lay the treasures of her lord, bronze and gold and iron well wrought. "— Butcher and Lang. Cf. "Od. " ii. 337; "Il. " vi. 288.

Next I proceeded to point out to her the several dwelling-rooms, all beautifully fitted up for cool in summer and for warmth in winter.

[3] I showed her how the house enjoyed a southern aspect, whence it was plain, in winter it would catch the sunlight and in summer lie in shade. [4] Then I showed her the women's apartments, separated from the men's apartments by a bolted door, [5] whereby nothing from within could be conveyed without clandestinely, nor children born and bred by our domestics without our knowledge and consent[6]—no unimportant matter, since, if the act of rearing children tends to make good servants still more loyally disposed, [7] cohabiting but sharpens ingenuity for mischief in the bad.

[3] See "Mem. " III. viii. 8.

[4] See "Mem. " ib. 9.

[5] "By bolts and bars. " Lit. "a door fitted with a bolt-pin. " See Thuc. ii. 4; Aristoph. "Wasps, " 200.

[6] Cf. (Aristot.) "Oecon. " i. 5, {dei de kai exomereuein tais teknopoiiais}.

[7] Lit. "since (you know) if the good sort of servant is rendered, as a rule, better disposed when he becomes a father, the base, through intermarrying, become only more ripe for mischief. "

When we had gone over all the rooms (he continued), we at once set about distribution our furniture[8] in classes; and we began (he said) by collecting everything we use in offering sacrifice. [9] After this we proceeded to set apart the ornaments and holiday attire of the wife, and the husband's clothing both for festivals and war; then the bedding used in the women's apartments, and the bedding used in the men's apartments; then the women's shoes and sandals, and the shoes and sandals of the men. [10] There was one division devoted to arms and armour; another to instruments used for carding wood; another to implements for making bread; another to utensils for cooking condiments; another to utensils for the bath; another connected with the kneading trough; another with the service of the table. All these we assigned to separate places, distinguishing one portion for daily and recurrent use and the rest for high days and holidays. Next we selected and set aside the supplies required for the month's expenditure; and, under a separate head, [11] we stored away what we computed would be needed for the year. [12] For in this way there is less chance of failing to note how the supplies are likely to last to the end.

The Economist

[8] "Movable property, " "meubles. "

[9] Holden cf. Plut. "De Curios. " 515 E, {os gar Xenophon legei toi Oikonomikois, k.t. l.}

[10] Cf. "Cyrop. " VIII. ii. 5. See Becker, op. cit. p. 447.

[11] See Cic. ap. Col. who curiously mistranslates {dikha}.

[12] Schneider, etc., cf. Aristot. "Oecon. " i. 6.

And so having arranged the different articles of furniture in classes, we proceeded to convey them to their appropriate places. That done, we directed our attention to the various articles needed by our domestics for daily use, such as implements or utensils for making bread, cooking relishes, spinning wool, and anything else of the same sort. These we consigned to the care of those who would have to use them, first pointing out where they must stow them, and enjoining on them to return them safe and sound when done with.

As to the other things which we should only use on feast-days, or for the entertainment of guests, or on other like occasions at long intervals, we delivered them one and all to our housekeeper. Having pointed out to her their proper places, and having numbered and registered[13] the several sets of articles, we explained that it was her business to give out each thing as required; to recollect to whom she gave them; and when she got them back, to restore them severally to the places from which she took them. In appointing our housekeeper, we had taken every pains to discover some one on whose self-restraint we might depend, not only in the matters of food and wine and sleep, but also in her intercourse with men. She must besides, to please us, be gifted with no ordinary memory. She must have sufficient forethought not to incur displeasure through neglect of our interests. It must be her object to gratify us in this or that, and in return to win esteem and honour at our hands. We set ourselves to teach and train her to feel a kindly disposition towards us, by allowing her to share our joys in the day of gladness, or, if aught unkind befell us, by inviting her to sympathise in our sorrow. We sought to rouse in her a zeal for our interests, an eagerness to promote the increase of our estate, by making her intelligent of its affairs, and by giving her a share in our successes. We instilled in her a sense of justice and uprightness, by holding the just in higher honour than the unjust, and by pointing out that the lives of the righteous are richer and less servile than those of the unrighteous; and this was the position in which she found herself installed in our household. [14]

[13] Or, "having taken an inventory of the several sets of things. " Cf. "Ages. " i. 18; "Cyrop. " VII. iv. 12. See Newman, op. cit. i. 171.

[14] Or, "and this was the position in which we presently established her herself. "

And now, on the strength of all that we had done, Socrates (he added), I addressed my wife, explaining that all these things would fail of use unless she took in charge herself to see that the order of each several part was kept. Thereupon I taught her that in every well- constituted city the citizens are not content merely to pass good laws, but they further choose them guardians of the laws, [15] whose function as inspectors is to praise the man whose acts are law-abiding, or to mulct some other who offends against the law. Accordingly, I bade her believe that she, the mistress, was herself to play the part of guardian of the laws to her whole household, examining whenever it seemed good to her, and passing in review the several chattels, just as the officer in command of a garrison[16] musters and reviews his men. She must apply her scrutiny and see that everything was well, even as the Senate[17] tests the condition of the Knights and of their horses. [18] Like a queen, she must bestow, according to the power vested in her, praise and honour on the well- deserving, but blame and chastisement on him who stood in need thereof.

[15] See Plat. "Laws, " vi. 755 A, 770 C; Aristot. "Pol. " iii. 15, 1287 A; iv. 14, 1298 B; vi. 8, 1323 A; "Ath. Pol. " viii. 4; and Cic. ap. Col. xii. 3. 10 f. Holden cf. Cic. "de Legg. " iii. 20, S. 46; "C. I. G. " 3794.

[16] Lit. Phrourarch, "the commandant. "

[17] Or, "Council" at Athens.

[18] Cf. "Hipparch. " i. 8, 13.

Nor did my lessons end here (added he); I taught her that she must not be annoyed should I seem to be enjoining upon her more trouble than upon any of our domestics with regard to our possessions; pointing out to her that these domestics have only so far a share in their master's chattels that they must fetch and carry, tend and guard them; nor have they the right to use a single one of them except the master grant it. But to the master himself all things pertain to use as he thinks best. And so I pointed the conclusion: he to whom the greater gain attaches in the preservation of the property or loss in its destruction, is surely he to whom by right belongs the larger measure of attention. [19]

[19] Or, "he it is on whom devolves as his concern the duty of surveillance."

When, then (I asked), Ischomachus, how fared it? was your wife disposed at all to lend a willing ear to what you told her? [20]

[20] Lit. "when she heard did she give ear at all?"

Bless you, [21] Socrates (he answered), what did she do but forthwith answer me, I formed a wrong opinion if I fancied that, in teaching her the need of minding our property, I was imposing a painful task upon her. A painful task it might have been[22] (she added), had I bade her neglect her personal concerns! But to be obliged to fulfil the duty of attending to her own domestic happiness, [23] that was easy. After all it would seem to be but natural (added he); just as any honest[24] woman finds it easier to care for her own offspring than to neglect them, so, too, he could well believe, an honest woman might find it pleasanter to care for than to neglect possessions, the very charm of which is that they are one's very own.

[21] Lit. "By Hera!" Cf. the old formula "Marry!" or "By'r lakin!"

[22] Lit. "more painful had it been, had I enjoined her to neglect her own interests than to be obliged . .. "

[23] {ton oikeion agathon}, cp. "charity begins at home." See Joel, op. cit. p. 448.

[24] Or, "true and honest"; "any woman worthy of the name." {sophroni} = with the {sophrosune} of womanhood; possibly transl. "discreet and sober-minded."

X

So (continued Socrates), when I heard his wife had made this answer, I exclaimed: By Hera, Ischomachus, a brave and masculine intelligence the lady has, as you describe her.

(To which Ischomachus) Yes, Socrates, and I would fain narrate some other instances of like large-mindedness on her part: shown in the readiness with which she listened to my words and carried out my wishes.

What sort of thing? (I answered). Do, pray, tell me, since I would far more gladly learn about a living woman's virtues than that Zeuxis[1] should show me the portrait of the loveliest woman he has painted.

[1] See "Mem. " I. iv. 3.

Whereupon Ischomachus proceeded to narrate as follows: I must tell you, Socrates, I one day noticed she was much enamelled with white lead, [2] no doubt to enhance the natural whitenes of her skin; she had rouged herself with alkanet[3] profusely, doubtless to give more colour to her cheeks than truth would warrant; she was wearing high- heeled shoes, in order to seem taller than she was by nature. [4]

[2] Cf. Aristoph. "Eccl. " 878; ib. 929, {egkhousa mallon kai to son psimuthion}: ib. 1072; "Plut. " 1064.

[3] Lit. "enamelled or painted with anchusa or alkanet, " a plant, the wild bugloss, whose root yields a red dye. Cf. Aristoph. "Lys. " 48; Theophr. "H. Pl. " vii. 8. 3.

[4] See Becker, op. cit. p. 452; Breit. cf. "Anab. " III. ii. 25; "Mem. " II. i. 22; Aristot. "Eth. Nic. " iv. 3, 5, "True beauty requires a great body. "

Accordingly I put to her this question: [5] "Tell me, my wife, would you esteem me a less lovable co-partner in our wealth, were I to show you how our fortune stands exactly, without boasting of unreal possessions or concealing what we really have? Or would you prefer that I should try to cheat you with exaggeration, exhibiting false money to you, or sham[6] necklaces, or flaunting purples[7] which will lose their colour, stating they are genuine the while? "

[5] Lit. "So I said to her, 'Tell me, my wife, after which fashion would you find me the more delectable partner in our joint estate — were I to . . .? or were I to . . .?'"

[6] Lit. "only wood coated with gold."

[7] See Becker, op. cit. p. 434 f; Holden cf. Athen. ix. 374, xii. 525; Ael. "V. H." xii. 32; Aristoph. "Plut." 533.

She caught me up at once: "Hush, hush!" she said, "talk not such talk. May heaven forfend that you should ever be like that. I could not love you with my whole heart were you really of that sort."

"And are we two not come together," I continued, "for a closer partnership, being each a sharer in the other's body?"

"That, at any rate, is what folk say," she answered.

"Then as regards this bodily relation," I proceeded, "should you regard me as more lovable or less did I present myself, my one endeavour and my sole care being that my body should be hale and strong and thereby well complexioned, or would you have me first anoint myself with pigments, [8] smear my eyes with patches[9] of 'true flesh colour,'[10] and so seek your embrace, like a cheating consort presenting to his mistress's sight and touch vermillion paste instead of his own flesh?"

[8] "Red lead."

[9] Cf. Aristoph. "Ach." 1029.

[10] {andreikelon}. Cf. Plat. "Rep." 501 B, "the human complexion"; "Crat." 424 E.

"Frankly," she answered, "it would not please me better to touch paste than your true self. Rather would I see your own 'true flesh colour' than any pigment of that name; would liefer look into your eyes and see them radiant with health than washed with any wash, or dyed with any ointment there may be."

"Believe the same, my wife, of me then," Ischomachus continued (so he told me); "believe that I too am not better pleased with white enamel or with alkanet than with your own natural hue; but as the gods have fashioned horses to delight in horses, cattle in cattle, sheep in their fellow sheep, so to human beings the human body pure and undefiled is sweetest; [11] and as to these deceits, though they may serve to cheat the outside world without detection, yet if intimates try to deceive each other, they must one day be caught; in rising from their beds, before they make their toilet; by a drop of sweat they stand convicted; tears are an ordeal they cannot pass; the bath reveals them as they truly are."

[11] See "Mem." II. i. 22.

What answer (said I) did she make, in Heaven's name, to what you said?

What, indeed (replied the husband), save only, that thenceforward she never once indulged in any practice of the sort, but has striven to display the natural beauty of her person in its purity. She did, however, put to me a question: Could I advise her how she might become not in false show but really fair to look upon?

This, then, was the counsel which I gave her, Socrates: Not to be for ever seated like a slave; [12] but, with Heaven's help, to assume the attitude of a true mistress standing before the loom, and where her knowledge gave her the superiority, bravely to give the aid of her instruction; where her knowledge failed, as bravely try to learn. I counselled her to oversee the baking woman as she made the bread; to stand beside the housekeeper as she measured out her stores; to go tours of inspection to see if all things were in order as they should be. For, as it seemed to me, this would at once be walking exercise and supervision. And, as an excellent gymnastic, I recommended her to knead the dough and roll the paste; to shake the coverlets and make the beds; adding, if she trained herself in exercise of this sort she would enjoy her food, grow vigorous in health, and her complexion would in very truth be lovelier. The very look and aspect of the wife, the mistress, seen in rivalry with that of her attendants, being as she is at once more fair[13] and more beautifully adorned, has an attractive charm, [14] and not the less because her acts are acts of grace, not services enforced. Whereas your ordinary fine lady, seated in solemn state, would seem to court comparison with painted counterfeits of womanhood.

[12] See Becker, p. 491. Breit., etc., cf. Nicostr. ap. Stob. "Tit." lxxiv. 61.

[13] Lit. "more spotles"; "like a diamond of purest water. " Cf. Shakesp. "Lucr. " 394, "whose perfect white Showed like an April daisy in the grass. "

[14] Or, "is wondrous wooing, and all the more with this addition, hers are acts of grace, theirs services enforced. "

And, Socrates, I would have you know that still to-day, my wife is living in a style as simple as that I taught her then, and now recount to you.

XI

The conversation was resumed as follows: Thanking Ischomachus for what he had told me about the occupations of his wife; on that side I have heard enough (I said) perhaps for a beginning; the facts you mention reflect the greatest credit on both wife and husband; but would you now in turn describe to me your work and business? In doing so you will have the pleasure of narrating the reason of your fame. And I, for my part, when I have heard from end to end the story of a beautiful and good man's works, if only my wits suffice and I have understood it, shall be much indebted.

Indeed (replied Ischomachus), it will give me the greatest pleasure to recount to you my daily occupations, and in return I beg you to reform me, where you find some flaw or other in my conduct. [1]

[1] Lit. "in order that you on your side may correct and set me right where I seem to you to act amiss. " {metarruthmises}—remodel. Cf. Aristot. "Nic. Eth. " x. 9. 5.

The idea of my reforming you! (I said). How could I with any show of justice hope to reform you, the perfect model[2] of a beautiful, good man—I, who am but an empty babbler, [3] and measurer of the air, [4] who have to bear besides that most senseless imputation of being poor —an imputation which, I assure you, Ischomachus, would have reduced me to the veriest despair, except that the other day I chanced to come across the horse of Nicias, [5] the foreigner? I saw a crowd of people in attendance staring, and I listened to a story which some one had to tell about the animal. So then I stepped up boldly to the groom and asked him, "Has the horse much wealth? " The fellow looked at me as if I were hardly in my right mind to put the question, and retorted, "How can a horse have wealth? " Thereat I dared to lift my eyes from earth, on learning that after all it is permitted a poor penniless horse to be a noble animal, if nature only have endowed him with good spirit. If, therefore, it is permitted even to me to be a good man, please recount to me your works from first to last, I promise, I will listen, all I can, and try to understand, and so far as in me lies to imitate you from to-morrow. To-morrow is a good day to commence a course of virtue, is it not?

[2] Cf. Plat. "Rep. " 566 A, "a tyrant full grown" (Jowett).

[3] Cf. Plat. "Phaed. " 70 C; Aristoph. "Clouds, " 1480.

[4] Or rather, "a measurer of air"—i. e. devoted not to good sound solid "geometry, " but the unsubstantial science of "aerometry. " See Aristoph. "Clouds, " i. 225; Plat. "Apol. " 18 B, 19 B; Xen. "Symp. " vi. 7.

[5] Nothing is known of this person.

You are pleased to jest, Socrates (Ischomachus replied), in spite of which I will recount to you those habits and pursuits by aid of which I seek to traverse life's course. If I have read aright life's lesson, it has taught me that, unless a man first discover what he needs to do, and seriously study to bring the same to good effect, the gods have placed prosperity[6] beyond his reach; and even to the wise and careful they give or they withhold good fortune as seemeth to them best. Such being my creed, I begin with service rendered to the gods; and strive to regulate my conduct so that grace may be given me, in answer to my prayers, to attain to health, and strength of body, honour in my own city, goodwill among my friends, safety with renown in war, and of riches increase, won without reproach.

[6] "The gods have made well-doing and well-being a thing impossible. " Cf. "Mem. " III. ix. 7, 14.

I, when I heard these words, replied: And are you then indeed so careful to grow rich, Ischomachus? —amassing wealth but to gain endless trouble in its management?

Most certainly (replied Ischomachus), and most careful must I needs be of the things you speak of. So sweet I find it, Socrates, to honour God magnificently, to lend assistance to my friends in answer to their wants, and, so far as lies within my power, not to leave my city unadorned with anything which riches can bestow.

Nay (I answered), beautiful indeed the works you speak of, and powerful the man must be who would essay them. How can it be otherwise, seeing so many human beings need the help of others merely to carry on existence, and so many are content if they can win enough to satisfy their wants. What of those therefore who are able, not only to administer their own estates, but even to create a surplus sufficient to adorn their city and relieve the burthen of their friends? Well may we regard such people as men of substance and capacity.

The Economist

But stay (I added), most of us are competent to sing the praises of such heroes. What I desire is to hear from you, Ischomachus, in your own order, [7] first how you study to preserve your health and strength of body; and next, how it is granted to you[8] to escape from the perils of war with honour untarnished. And after that (I added), it will much content me to learn from your own lips about your money-making.

[7] "And from your own starting-point."

[8] As to the construction {themis einai} see Jebb ad "Oed. Col." 1191, Appendix.

Yes (he answered), and the fact is, Socrates, if I mistake not, all these matters are in close connection, each depending on the other. Given that a man have a good meal to eat, he has only to work off the effect by toil[9] directed rightly; and in the process, if I mistake not, his health will be confirmed, his strength added to. Let him but practise the arts of war and in the day of battle he will preserve his life with honour. He needs only to expend his care aright, sealing his ears to weak and soft seductions, and his house shall surely be increased. [10]

[9] See "Mem." I. ii. 4; "Cyrop." I. ii. 16. Al. "bring out the effect of it by toil."

[10] Lit. "it is likely his estate will increase more largely."

I answered: So far I follow you, Ischomachus. You tell me that by labouring to his full strength, [11] by expending care, by practice and training, a man may hope more fully to secure life's blessings. So I take your meaning. But now I fain would learn of you some details. What particular toil do you impose on yourself in order to secure good health and strength? After what particular manner do you practise the arts of war? How do you take pains to create a surplus which will enable you to benefit your friends and to gratify the state?

[11] Or, "by working off ill-humours," as we should say.

Why then (Ischomachus replied), my habit is to rise from bed betimes, when I may still expect to find at home this, that, or the other friend, whom I may wish to see. Then, if anything has to be done in town, I set off to transact the business and make that my

The Economist

walk; [12] or, if there is no business to do in town, my serving-boy leads my horse to the farm; I follow, and so make the country-road my walk, which suits my purpose quite as well, or better, Socrates, perhaps, than pacing up and down the colonade. [13] Then when I have reached the farm, where mayhap some of my men are planting trees, or breaking fallow, sowing or getting in the crops, I inspect their various labours with an eye to every detail, and, whenever I can improve upon the present system, I introduce reform. After this, as a rule, I mount my horse and take a canter. I put him through his paces, suiting these, as far as possible, to those inevitable in war[14]—in other words, I avoid neither steep slope[15] nor sheer incline, neither trench nor runnel, only giving my utmost heed the while so as not to lame my horse while exercising him. When that is over, the boy gives the horse a roll, [16] and leads him homewards, taking at the same time from the country to town whatever we may chance to need. Meanwhile I am off for home, partly walking, partly running, and having reached home I take a bath and give myself a rub; [17] and then I breakfast—a repast which leaves me neither empty nor replete, [18] and will suffice to last me through the day.

[12] See "Mem. " III. xiii. 5.

[13] {xusto}—the xystus, "a covered corrider in the gymnasium where the athletes exercised in winter. " Vitruv. v. 11. 4; vi. 7. 5. See Rich, "Companion, " s. n.; Becker, op. cit. p. 309. Cf. Plat. "Phaedr. " 227—Phaedrus loq. : "I have come from Lysias the son of Cephalus, and I am going to take a walk outside the wall, for I have been sitting with him the whole morning; and our common friend Acumenus advises me to walk in the country, which he says is more invigorating than to walk in the courts. "—Jowett.

[14] See "Horsemanship, " iii. 7 foll. ; ib. viii. ; "Hipparch, " i. 18.

[15] "Slanting hillside. "

[16] See "Horsemanship, " v. 3; Aristoph. "Clouds, " 32.

[17] Lit. "scrape myself clean" (with the {stleggis} or strigil. Cf. Aristoph. "Knights, " 580. See Becker, op. cit. p. 150.

[18] See "Lac. Pol. " ii. 5. Cf. Hor. "Sat. " i. 6. 127:

pransus non avide, quantum interpellet inani ventre diem durare.

Then eat a temperate luncheon, just to stay A sinking stomach till the close of day (Conington).

By Hera (I replied), Ischomachus, I cannot say how much your doings take my fancy. How you have contrived, to pack up portably for use— together at the same time—appliances for health and recipes for strength, exercises for war, and pains to promote your wealth! My admiration is raised at every point. That you do study each of these pursuits in the right way, you are yourself a standing proof. Your look of heaven-sent health and general robustness we note with our eyes, while our ears have heard your reputation as a first-rate horseman and the wealthiest of men.

Isch. Yes, Socrates, such is my conduct, in return for which I am rewarded with—the calumnies of half the world. You thought, I daresay, I was going to end my sentence different, and say that a host of people have given me the enviable title "beautiful and good."

I was indeed myself about to ask, Ischomachus (I answered), whether you take pains also to acquire skill in argumentative debate, the cut and thrust and parry of discussion, [19] should occasion call?

[19] Lit. "to give a reason and to get a reason from others. " Cf. "Cyrop. " I. iv. 3.

Isch. Does it not strike you rather, Socrates, that I am engaged in one long practice of this very skill, [20] now pleading as defendant that, as far as I am able, I do good to many and hurt nobody? And then, again, you must admit, I play the part of prosecutor when accusing people whom I recognise to be offenders, as a rule in private life, or possibly against the state, the good-for-nothing fellows?

[20] "The arts of the defendant, the apologist; and of the plaintiff, the prosecutor. "

But please explain one other thing, Ischomachus (I answered). Do you put defence and accusation into formal language? [21]

[21] "Does your practice include the art of translating into words your sentiments? " Cf. "Mem. " I. ii. 52.

The Economist

Isch. "Formal language, " say you, Socrates? The fact is, I never cease to practise speaking; and on this wise: Some member of my household has some charge to bring, or some defence to make, [22] against some other. I have to listen and examine. I must try to sift the truth. Or there is some one whom I have to blame or praise before my friends, or I must arbitrate between some close connections and endeavour to enforce the lesson that it is to their own interests to be friends not foes. [23] . .. We are present to assist a general in court; [24] we are called upon to censure some one; or defend some other charged unjustly; or to prosecute a third who has received an honour which he ill deserves. It frequently occurs in our debates[25] that there is some course which we strongly favour: naturally we sound its praises; or some other, which we disapprove of: no less naturally we point out its defects.

[22] Or, "One member of my household appears as plaintiff, another as defendant. I must listen and cross-question. "

[23] The "asyndeton" would seem to mark a pause, unless some words have dropped out. See the commentators ad loc.

[24] The scene is perhaps that of a court-martial (cf. "Anab. " V. viii. ; Dem. "c. Timocr. " 749. 16). (Al. cf. Sturz, "Lex. " s. v. "we are present (as advocates) and censure some general"), or more probably, I think, that of a civil judicial inquiry of some sort, conducted at a later date by the Minister of Finance ({to stratego to epi tas summorias eremeno}).

[25] Or, "Or again, a frequent case, we sit in council" (as members of the Boule). See Aristot. "Pol. " iv. 15.

He paused, then added: Things have indeed now got so far, Socrates, that several times I have had to stand my trial and have judgment passed upon me in set terms, what I must pay or what requital I must make. [26]

[26] See "Symp. " v. 8. Al. {dielemmenos} = "to be taken apart and have . .. "

And at whose bar (I asked) is the sentence given? That point I failed to catch. [27]

[27] Or, "so dull was I, I failed to catch the point. "

The Economist

Whose but my own wife's? (he answered).

And, pray, how do you conduct your own case? (I asked). [28]

[28] See "Mem. " III. vii. 4; Plat. "Euth. " 3 E.

Not so ill (he answered), when truth and interest correspond, but when they are opposed, Socrates, I have no skill to make the worse appear the better argument. [29]

[29] See Plat. "Apol. " 19-23 D; Aristoph. "Clouds, " 114 foll.

Perhaps you have no skill, Ischomachus, to make black white or falsehood truth (said I). [30]

[30] Or, "It may well be, Ischomachus, you cannot manufacture falsehood into truth. " Lit. "Like enough you cannot make an untruth true. "

XII

But (I continued presently), perhaps I am preventing you from going, as you long have wished to do, Ischomachus?

To which he: By no means, Socrates. I should not think of going away until the gathering in the market is dispersed. [1]

[1] Lit. "until the market is quite broken up, " i. e. after mid-day. See "Anab. " I. viii. 1; II. i. 7; "Mem. " I. i. 10. Cf. Herod. ii. 173; iii. 104; vii. 223.

Of course, of course (I answered), you are naturally most careful not to forfeit the title they have given you of "honest gentleman"; [2] and yet, I daresay, fifty things at home are asking your attention at this moment; only you undertook to meet your foreign friends, and rather than play them false you go on waiting.

[2] Lit. "beautiful and good. "

Isch. Let me so far corect you, Socrates; in no case will the things you speak of be neglected, since I have stewards and bailiffs[3] on the farms.

[3] Cf. Becker, op. cit. p. 363.

Soc. And, pray, what is your system when you need a bailiff? Do you search about, until you light on some one with a natural turn for stewardship; and then try to purchase him? —as, I feel certain, happens when you want a carpenter: first, you discover some one with a turn for carpentry, and then do all you can to get possession of him. [4] Or do you educate your bailiffs yourself?

[4] The steward, like the carpenter, and the labourers in general, would, as a rule, be a slave. See below, xxi. 9.

Isch. Most certainly the latter, Socrates; I try to educate them, as you say, myself; and with good reason. He who is properly to fill my place and manage my affairs when I am absent, my "alter ego, "[5] needs but to have my knowledge; and if I am fit myself to stand at the head of my own business, I presume I should be able to put another in possession of my knowledge. [6]

[5] Or, "my other self."

[6] Lit. "to teach another what I know myself."

Soc. Well then, the first thing he who is properly to take your place when absent must possess is goodwill towards you and yours; for without goodwill, what advantage will there be in any knowledge whatsoever which your bailiff may possess?

Isch. None, Socrates; and I may tell you that a kindly disposition towards me and mine is precisely what I first endeavour to instil.

Soc. And how, in the name of all that is holy, do you pick out whom you will and teach him to have kindly feeling towards yourself and yours?

Isch. By kindly treatment of him, to be sure, whenever the gods bestow abundance of good things upon us.

Soc. If I take your meaning rightly, you would say that those who enjoy your good things grow well disposed to you and seek to render you some good?

Isch. Yes, for of all instruments to promote good feeling this I see to be the best.

Soc. Well, granted the man is well disposed to you does it therefore follow, Ischomachus, that he is fit to be your bailiff? It cannot have escaped your observation that albeit human beings, as a rule, are kindly disposed towards themselves, yet a large number of them will not apply the attention requisite to secure for themselves those good things which they fain would have.

Isch. Yes, but believe me, Socrates, when I seek to appoint such men as bailiffs, I teach them also carefulness and application. [7]

[7] {epimeleia} is a cardinal virtue with the Greeks, or at any rate with Xenophon, but it has no single name in English.

Soc. Nay, now in Heaven's name, once more, how can that be? I always thought it was beyond the power of any teacher to teach these virtues. [8]

[8] For the Socratic problem {ei arete didakte} see Grote, "H. G." viii. 599.

Isch. Nor is it possible, you are right so far, to teach such excellences to every single soul in order as simply as a man might number off his fingers.

Soc. Pray, then, what sort of people have the privilege? [9] Should you mind pointing them out to me with some distinctness?

[9] Lit. "what kind of people can be taught them? By all means signify the sort to me distinctly."

Ishc. Well, in the first place, you would have some difficulty in making intemperate people diligent—I speak of intemperance with regard to wine, for drunkenness creates forgetfulness of everything which needs to be done.

Soc. And are persons devoid of self-control in this respect the only people incapable of diligence and carefulness? or are there others in like case?

Isch. Certainly, people who are intemperate with regard to sleep, seeing that the sluggard with his eyes shut cannot do himself or see that others do what is right.

Soc. What then? [10] Are we to regard these as the only people incapable of being taught this virtue of carefulness? or are there others in a like condition?

[10] Or, "What then—is the list exhausted? Are we to suppose that these are the sole people . .. "

Isch. Surely we must include the slave to amorous affection. [11] Your woeful lover[12] is incapable of being taught attention to anything beyond one single object. [13] No light task, I take it, to discover any hope or occupation sweeter to him than that which now employs him, his care for his beloved, nor, when the call for action comes, [14] will it be easy to invent worse punishment than that he now endures in separation from the object of his passion. [15] Accordingly, I am in no great hurry to appoint a person of this sort to manage[16] my affairs; the very attempt to do so I regard as futile.

[11] See "Mem. " I. iii. 8 foll. ; II. vi. 22.

[12] {duserotes}. Cf. Thuc. vi. 13, "a desperate craving" (Jowett).

[13] Cf. "Symp. " iv. 21 foll. ; "Cyrop. " V. i. 7-18.

[14] Or, "where demands of business present themselves, and something must be done. "

[15] Cf. Shakesp. "Sonnets, " passim.

[16] Or, "I never dream of appointing as superintendent. " See above, iv. 7.

Soc. Well, and what of those addicted to another passion, that of gain? Are they, too, incapable of being trained to give attention to field and farming operations?

Isch. On the contrary, there are no people easier to train, none so susceptible of carefulness in these same matters. One needs only to point out to them that the pursuit is gainful, and their interest is aroused.

Soc. But for ordinary people? Given they are self-controlled to suit your bidding, [17] given they possess a wholesome appetite for gain, how will you lesson them in carefulness? how teach them growth in diligence to meet your wishes?

[17] Or, "in matters such as you insist on. "

Isch. By a simple method, Socrates. When I see a man intent on carefulness, I praise and do my best to honour him. When, on the other hand, I see a man neglectful of his duties, I do not spare him: I try in every way, by word and deed, to wound him.

Soc. Come now, Ischomachus, kindly permit a turn in the discussion, which has hitherto concerned the persons being trained to carefulness themselves, and explain a point in reference to the training process. Is it possible for a man devoid of carefulness himself to render others more careful?

No more possible (he answered) than for a man who knows no music to make others musical. [18] If the teacher sets but an ill

The Economist

example, the pupil can hardly learn to do the thing aright. [19] And if the master's conduct is suggestive of laxity, how hardly shall his followers attain to carefulness! Or to put the matter concisely, "like master like man. " I do not think I ever knew or heard tell of a bad master blessed with good servants. The converse I certainly have seen ere now, a good master and bad servants; but they were the sufferers, not he. [20] No, he who would create a spirit of carefulness in others[21] must have the skill himself to supervise the field of labour; to test, examine, scrutinise. [22] He must be ready to requite where due the favour of a service well performed, nor hesitate to visit the penalty of their deserts upon those neglectful of their duty. [23] Indeed (he added), the answer of the barbarian to the king seems aposite. You know the story, [24] how the king had met with a good horse, but wished to give the creature flesh and that without delay, and so asked some one reputed to be clever about horses: "What will give him flesh most quickly? " To which the other: "The master's eye. " So, too, it strikes me, Socrates, there is nothing like "the master's eye" to call forth latent qualities, and turn the same to beautiful and good effect. [25]

[18] Or, "to give others skill in 'music. '" See Plat. "Rep. " 455 E; "Laws, " 802 B. Al. "a man devoid of letters to make others scholarly. " See Plat. "Phaedr. " 248 D.

[19] Lit. "when the teacher traces the outline of the thing to copy badly. " For {upodeiknuontos} see "Mem. " IV. iii. 13; "Horsem. " ii. 2. Cf. Aristot. "Oecon. " i. 6; "Ath. Pol. " 41. 17; and Dr. Sandys' note ad loc.

[20] Or, "but they did not go scot-free"; "punishments then were rife. "

[21] Cf. Plat. "Polit. " 275 E: "If we say either tending the herds, or managing the herds, or having the care of them, that will include all, and then we may wrap up the statesman with the rest, as the argument seems to require. " — Jowett.

[22] Or, "he must have skill to over-eye the field of labour, and be scrutinous. "

[23] "For every boon of service well performed he must be eager to make requital to the author of it, nor hesitate to visit on the heads of those neglectful of their duty a just recompense. " (The language is poetical.)

The Economist

[24] See Aristot. "Oecon. " i. 6; Aesch. "Pers. " 165; Cato ap. Plin. "H. N." xviii. 5. Cic. ap. Colum. iv. 18; ib. vi. 21; La Fontaine, "L'Oeil du Maitre. "

[25] Or, "so, too, in general it seems to me 'the master's eye' is aptest to elicit energy to issue beautiful and good. "

XIII

But now (I ventured), suppose you have presented strongly to the mind of some one[1] the need of carefulness to execute your wishes, is a person so qualified to be regarded as fit at once to be your bailiff? or is there aught else which he must learn in order to play the part of an efficient bailiff?

[1] Breit. cf. "Pol. Lac. " xv. 8. Holden cf. Plat. "Rep. " 600 C.

Most certainly there is (he answered): it still remains for him to learn particulars—to know, that is, what things he has to do, and when and how to do them; or else, if ignorant of these details, the profit of this bailiff in the abstract may prove no greater than the doctor's who pays a most precise attention to a sick man, visiting him late and early, but what will serve to ease his patient's pains[2] he knows not.

[2] Lit. "what it is to the advantage of his patient to do, is beyond his ken. "

Soc. But suppose him to have learnt the whole routine of business, will he need aught else, or have we found at last your bailiff absolute? [3]

[3] Cf. Plat. "Rep. " 566 D. Or, "the perfect and consummate type of bailiff. "

Isch. He must learn at any rate, I think, to rule his fellow-workmen.

What! (I exclaimed): you mean to say you educate your bailiffs to that extent? Actually you make them capable of rule?

At any rate I try to do so (he replied).

And how, in Heaven's name (I asked), do you contrive to educate another in the skill to govern human beings?

Isch. I have a very simple system, Socrates; so simple, I daresay, you will simply laugh at me.

The Economist

Soc. The matter, I protest, is hardly one for laughter. The man who can make another capable of rule, clearly can teach him how to play the master; and if can make him play the master, he can make him what is grander still, a kingly being. [4] Once more, therefore, I protest: A man possessed of such creative power is worthy, not of ridicule, far from it, but of the highest praise.

[4] i. e. {arkhikos} includes (1) {despotikos}, i.e. an arbitrary head of any sort, from the master of one's own family to the {turannos kai despotes} (Plat. "Laws, " 859 A), despotic lord or owner; (2) {basilikos}, the king or monarch gifted with regal qualities.

Thus, then, I reason, [5] Socrates (he answered): The lower animals are taught obedience by two methods chiefly, partly through being punished when they make attempts to disobey, partly by experiencing some kindness when they cheerfully submit. This is the principle at any rate adopted in the breaking of young horses. The animal obeys its trainer, and something sweet is sure to follow; or it disobeys, and in place of something sweet it finds a peck of trouble; and so on, until it comes at last to yield obedience to the trainer's every wish. Or to take another instance: Young dogs, [6] however far inferior to man in thought and language, [7] can still be taught to run on errands and turn somersaults, [8] and do a host of other clever things, precisely on this same principle of training. Every time the animal obeys it gets something or other which it wanted, and every time it misbehaves it gets a whipping. But when it comes to human beings: in man you have a creature still more open to persuasion through appeals to reason; [9] only make it plain to him "it is his interest to obey. " Or if they happen to be slaves, [10] the more ignoble training of wild animals tamed to the lure will serve to teach obedience. Only gratify their bellies in the matter of appetite, and you will succeed in winning much from them. [11] But ambitious, emulous natures feel the spur of praise, [12] since some natures hunger after praise no less than others crave for meats and drinks. My practice then is to instruct those whom I desire to appoint as my bailiffs in the various methods which I have found myself to be successful in gaining the obedience of my fellows. To take an instance: There are clothes and shows and so forth, with which I must provide my workfolk. [13] Well, then, I see to it that these are not all alike in make; [14] but some will be of better, some of less good quality: my object being that these articles for use shall vary with the service of the wearer; the worse man will receive the worse things as a gift, the better man the better as a mark of honour. For I ask you, Socrates, how can the good avoid despondency seeing that the work is wrought by their own hands alone, in spite of which these villains who will neither labour nor face danger when occasion calls are to receive an equal guerdon with themselves? And just as I cannot bring myself in any sort of way to look upon the better sort as worthy to receive no greater honour than the baser, so, too, I praise my bailiffs when I know they have apportioned the best things among the most deserving. And if I see that some one is receiving preference by dint of flatteries or like unworthy means, I do not let the matter pass; I reprimand my bailiff roundly, and so teach him that such conduct is not even to his interest.

[5] {oukoun}. "This, then, is my major premiss: the dumb animal . .. " (lit. "the rest of animals").

[6] {ta kunidia} possibly implies "performing poodles."

[7] {te gnome . .. te glotte}, i.e. mental impression and expression, "mind and tongue."

[8] Or, "to run round and round and turn heels over head." Al. "dive for objects."

[9] "Logic, argument." Or, "a creature more compliant; merely by a word demonstrate to him . .. "

[10] Cf. Plat. "Rep." 591 C.

[11] See Pater, "Plato and Platonism," "Lacedaemon," p. 196 foll.

[12] See "Cyrop." passim.

[13] {ergastersi}, Xenophontic for the common Attic {ergatais}. See Hold. ad loc. for similar forms, and cf. Rutherford, "New Phrynichus," 59.

[14] Cf. Aristot. "Oecon." i. 5 (where the thesis is developed further).

XIV

Soc. Well, then, Ischomachus, supposing the man is now so fit to rule that he can compel obedience, [1] is he, I ask once more, your bailiff absolute? or even though possessed of all the qualifications you have named, does he still lack something? [2]

[1] Or, "that discipline flows from him; " al. "he presents you with obedient servants. "

[2] Lit. "will he still need something further to complete him? "

Most certainly (replied Ischomachus). One thing is still required of him, and that is to hold aloof from property and goods which are his master's; he must not steal. Consider, this is the very person through whose hands the fruits and produce pass, and he has the audacity to make away with them! perhaps he does not leave enough to cover the expenses of the farming operations! Where would be the use of farming the land by help of such an overseer?

What (I exclaimed), can I believe my ears? You actually undertake to teach them virtue! What really, justice!

Isch. To be sure, I do. but it does not follow therefore that I find all equally apt to lend an ear to my instruction. However, what I do is this. I take a leaf now out of the laws of Draco and again another out of the laws of Solon, [3] and so essay to start my household on the path of uprightness. And indeed, if I mistake not (he proceeded), both those legislators enacted many of their laws expressly with a view to teaching this branch of justice. [4] It is written, "Let a man be punished for a deed of theft"; "Let whosoever is detected in the act be bound and thrown in prison"; "If he offer violence, [5] let him be put to death. " It is clear that the intention of the lawgivers in framing these enactments was to render the sordid love of gain[6] devoid of profit to the unjust person. What I do, therefore, is to cull a sample of their precepts, which I supplement with others from the royal code[7] where applicable; and so I do my best to shape the members of my household into the likeness of just men concerning that which passes through their hands. And now observe—the laws first mentioned act as penalties, deterrent to transgressors only; whereas the royal code aims higher: by it not only is the malefactor punished, but the righteous and just person is rewarded. [8] The result is, that many a man, beholding how the just grow ever wealthier than the unjust, albeit harbouring in his heart some covetous desires, is constant still to virtue. To abstain from unjust dealing is engrained in him. [9]

[3] Cobet, "Pros. Xen. " cf. Plut. "Solon, " xvii. {proton men oun tous Drakontos nomous aneile k. t.l. } "First, then, he repealed all Draco's laws, except those concerning homicide, because they were too severe and the punishments too great; for death was appointed for almost all offences, insomuch that those that were convicted of idleness were to die, and those that stole a cabbage or an apple to suffer even as villains that comitted sacrilege or murder" (Clough, i. 184). See Aul. Gell. "N. A." xi. 13.

[4] "The branch of justice which concerns us, viz. righteous dealing between man and man. "

[5] For this sense of {tous egkheirountas} cf. Thuc. iv. 121; "Hell. " IV. v. 16. Al. {dedesthai tous egkheirountas kai thanatousthai en tis alo poion} (Weiske), "let the attempt be punished with imprisonment"; "let him who is caught in the act be put to death. "

[6] Cf. Plat. "Laws, " 754 E.

[7] Or, "the royal laws, " i. e. of Persia. Cf. "Anab. " I. ix. 16; "Cyrop. " I. ii. 2, 3. Or possibly = "regal"; cf. Plat. "Minos, " 317 C; {to men orthon nomos esti basilikos}.

[8] Lit. "benefited. "

[9] Lit. "Whereby, beholding the just becoming wealthier than the unjust, many albeit covetous at heart themselves most constantly abide by abstinence from evil-doing. "

Those of my household (he proceeded) whom, in spite of kindly treatment, I perceive to be persistently bent on evil-doing, in the end I treat as desperate cases. Incurable self-seekers, [10] plain enough to see, whose aspiration lifts them from earth, so eager are they to be reckoned just men, not by reason only of the gain derivable from justice, but through passionate desire to deserve my praise— these in the end I treat as free-born men. I make them wealthy, and not with riches only, but in honour, as befits their gentle manliness. [11] For if,

Socrates, there be one point in which the man who thirsts for honour differs from him who thirsts for gain, it is, I think, in willingness to toil, face danger, and abstain from shameful gains—for the sake of honour only and fair fame. [12]

[10] Lit. "Those, on the other hand, whom I discover to be roused" (to honesty—not solely because honesty is the best policy).

[11] Or, "men of fair and noble type"; "true gentlemen. " This passage suggests the "silver lining to the cloud" of slavery.

[12] Cf. Hom. "Il. " ix. 413, {oleto men moi nostos, atar kleos aphthiton estai}, "but my fame shall be imperishable. "

XV

Soc. But now, suppose, Ischomachus, you have created in the soul of some one a desire for your welfare; have inspired in him not a mere passive interest, but a deep concern to help you to achieve prosperity; further, you have obtained for him a knowledge of the methods needed to give the operations of the field some measure of success; you have, moreover, made him capable of ruling; and, as the crowning point of all your efforts, this same trusty person shows no less delight, than you might take yourself, in laying at your feet[1] earth's products, each in due season richly harvested—I need hardly ask concerning such an one, whether aught else is lacking to him. It is clear to me[2] an overseer of this sort would be worth his weight in gold. But now, Ischomachus, I would have you not omit a topic somewhat lightly handled by us in the previous argument. [3]

[1] {apodeiknuon}, i.e. in presenting the inventory of products for the year. Cf. "Hell. " V. iii. 17; "Revenues, " ii. 7.

[2] {ede}, at this stage of the discussion.

[3] Or, "that part of the discussion which we ran over in a light and airy fashion, " in reference to xiii. 2.

What topic, pray, was that? (he asked).

Soc. You said, if I mistake not, that it was most important to learn the methods of conducting the several processes of husbandry; for, you added, unless a man knows what things he has to do and how to do them, all the care and diligence in the world will stand him in no stead.

At this point[4] he took me up, observing: So what you now command me is to teach the art itself of tillage, Socrates?

[4] Keeping the vulg. order of SS. 3-9, which many commentators would rearrange in various ways. See Breit. ad loc. ; Lincke, op. cit. p. 111 foll.

Yes (I replied), for now it looks as if this art were one which made the wise and skilled possessor of it wealthy, whilst the unskilled, in spite of all the pains he takes, must live in indigence.

Isch. Now shall you hear, then, [5] Socrates, the generous nature of this human art. For is it not a proof of something noble in it, that being of supreme utility, so sweet a craft to exercise, so rich in beauty, so acceptable alike to gods and men, the art of husbandry may further fairly claim to be the easiest of all the arts to learn? Noble I name it! this, at any rate, the epithet we give to animals which, being beautiful and large and useful, are also gentle towards the race of man. [6]

[5] Or, "Listen, then, and whilst I recount to you at once the loving-kindness of this art, to man the friendliest. "

[6] Schenkl regards this sentence as an interpolation. For the epithet {gennaios} applied to the dog see "Cyrop. " I. iv. 15, 21; "Hunting, " iv. 7.

Allow me to explain, Ischomachus (I interposed). Up to a certain point I fully followed what you said. I understand, according to your theory, how a bailiff must be taught. In other words, I follow your descriptions both as to how you make him kindly disposed towards yourself; and how, again, you make him careful, capable of rule, and upright. But at that point you made the statement that, in order to apply this diligence to tillage rightly, the careful husbandman must further learn what are the different things he has to do, and not alone what things he has to do, but how and when to do them. These are the topics which, in my opinion, have hitherto been somewhat lightly handled in the argument. Let me make my meaning clearer by an instance: it is as if you were to tell me that, in order to be able to take down a speech in writing, [7] or to read a written statement, a man must know his letters. Of course, if not stone deaf, I must have garnered that for a certain object knowledge of letters was important to me, but the bare recognition of the fact, I fear, would not enable me in any deeper sense to know my letters. So, too, at present I am easily persuaded that if I am to direct my care aright in tillage I must have a knowledge of the art of tillage. But the bare recognition of the fact does not one whit provide me with the knowledge how I ought to till. And if I resolved without ado to set about the work of tilling, I imagine, I should soon resemble your physician going on his rounds and visiting his patients without knowing what to prescribe or what to do to ease their sufferings. To save me from the like predicaments, please teach me the actual work and processes of tillage.

[7] Or, "something from dictation. "

The Economist

Isch. But truly, [8] Socrates, it is not with tillage as with the other arts, where the learner must be well-nigh crushed[9] beneath a load of study before his prentice-hand can turn out work of worth sufficient merely to support him. [10] The art of husbandry, I say, is not so ill to learn and cross-grained; but by watching labourers in the field, by listening to what they say, you will have straightway knowledge enough to teach another, should the humour take you. I imagine, Socrates (he added), that you yourself, albeit quite unconscious of the fact, already know a vast amount about the subject. The fact is, other craftsmen (the race, I mean, in general of artists) are each and all disposed to keep the most important[11] features of their several arts concealed: with husbandry it is different. Here the man who has the most skill in planting will take most pleasure in being watched by others; and so too the most skilful sower. Ask any question you may choose about results thus beautifully wrought, and not one feature in the whole performance will the doer of it seek to keep concealed. To such height of nobleness (he added), Socrats, does husbandry appear, like some fair mistress, to conform the soul and disposition of those concerned with it.

[8] "Nay, if you will but listen, Socrates, with husbandry it is not the same as with the other arts. "

[9] {katatribenai}, "worn out. " See "Mem. " III. iv. 1; IV. vii. 5. Al. "bored to death. "

[10] Or, "before the products of his pupilage are worth his keep. "

[11] Or, "critical and crucial. "

The proem[12] to the speech is beautiful at any rate (I answered), but hardly calculated to divert the hearer from the previous question. A thing so easy to be learnt, you say? then, if so, do you be all the readier for that reason to explain its details to me. No shame on you who teach, to teach these easy matters; but for me to lack the knowledge of them, and most of all if highly useful to the learner, worse than shame, a scandal.

[12] Or, "the prelude to the piece. "

XVI

Isch. First then, Socrates, I wish to demonstrate to you that what is called[1] "the intricate variety in husbandry"[2] presents no difficulty. I use a phrase of those who, whatever the nicety with which they treat the art in theory, [3] have but the faintest practical experience of tillage. What they assert is, that "he who would rightly till the soil must first be made acquainted with the nature of the earth."

[1] "They term"; in reference to the author of some treatise.

[2] Or, "the riddling subtlety of tillage." See "Mem." II. iii. 10; Plat. "Symp." 182 B; "Phileb." 53 E.

[3] Theophr. "De Caus." ii. 4, 12, mentions Leophanes amongst other writers on agriculture preceding himself.

And they are surely right in their assertion (I replied); for he who does not know what the soil is capable of bearing, can hardly know, I fancy, what he has to plant or what to sow.

But he has only to look at his neighbour's land (he answered), at his crops and trees, in order to learn what the soil can bear and what it cannot. [4] After which discovery, it is ill work fighting against heaven. Certainly not by dint of sowing and planting what he himself desires will he meet the needs of life more fully than by planting and sowing what the earth herself rejoices to bear and nourish on her bosom. Or if, as well may be the case, through the idleness of those who occupy it, the land itself cannot display its native faculty, [5] it is often possible to derive a truer notion from some neighbouring district that ever you will learn about it from your neighbour's lips. [6] Nay, even though the earth lie waste and barren, it may still declare its nature; since a soil productive of beautiful wild fruits can by careful tending be made to yield fruits of the cultivated kind as beautiful. And on this wise, he who has the barest knowledge[7] of the art of tillage can still discern the nature of the soil.

[4] Holden cf. Virg. "Georg." i. 53; iv. 109. According to the commentator Servius, the poet drew largely upon Xenophon's treatise.

The Economist

[5] Or, "cannot prove its natural aptitude."

[6] Or, "from a neighbouring mortal."

[7] Or, "a mere empiric in the art of husbandry."

Thank you (I said), Ischomachus, my courage needs no further fanning upon that score. I am bold enough now to believe that no one need abstain from agriculture for fear he will not recognise the nature of the soil. Indeed, I now recall to mind a fact concerning fishermen, how as they ply their business on the seas, not crawling lazily along, nor bringing to, for prospect's sake, but in the act of scudding past the flying farmsteads, [8] these brave mariners have only to set eyes upon crops on land, and they will boldly pronounce opinion on the nature of the soil itself, whether good or bad: this they blame and that they praise. And these opinions for the most part coincide, I notice, with the verdict of the skilful farmer as to quality of soil. [9]

[8] Or, "the flying coastland, fields and farmyards."

[9] Lit. "And indeed the opinions they pronounce about 'a good soil' mostly tally with the verdict of the expert farmer."

Isch. At what point shall I begin then, Socrates, to revive your recollection[10] of the art of husbandry? since to explain to you the processes employed in husbandry means the statement of a hundred details which you know yourself full well already.

[10] Or, "begin recalling to your mind." See Plat. "Meno," for the doctrine of Anamensis here apparently referred to.

Soc. The first thing I should like to learn, Ischomachus, I think, if only as a point befitting a philosopher, is this: how to proceed and how to work the soil, did I desire to extract the largest crops of wheat and barley.

Isch. Good, then! you are aware that fallow must be broken up in readiness[11] for sowing?

[11] Or, "ploughed up." Cf. Theophr. "Hist. Pl." iii. i. 6; Dion. Hal. "Ant." x. 17.

The Economist

Soc. Yes, I am aware of that.

Isch. Well then, supposing we begin to plough our land in winter?

Soc. It would not do. There would be too much mud.

Isch. Well then, what would you say to summer?

Soc. The soil will be too hard in summer for a plough and a pair of oxen to break up.

Isch. It looks as if spring-time were the season to begin this work, then? What do you say?

Soc. I say, one may expect the soil broken up at that season of the year to crumble[12] best.

[12] {kheisthai} = laxari, dissolvi, to be most friable, to scatter readily.

Isch. Yes, and grasses[13] turned over at that season, Socrates, serve to supply the soil already with manure; while as they have not shed their seed as yet, they cannot vegetate. [14] I am supposing that you recognise a further fact: to form good land, a fallow must be clean and clear of undergrowth and weeds, [15] and baked as much as possible by exposure to the sun. [16]

[13] "Herbage, " whether grass or other plants, "grass, " "clover, " etc; Theophr. "Hist. Pl. " i. 3. 1; Holden, "green crops. "

[14] Lit. "and not as yet have shed their seed so as to spring into blade. "

[15] Or, "quitch. "

[16] Holden cf. Virg. "Georg. " i. 65, coquat; ii. 260, excoquere. So Lucr. vi. 962.

Soc. Yes, that is quite a proper state of things, I should imagine.

Isch. And to bring about this proper state of things, do you maintain there can be any other better system than that of turning the soil over as many times as possible in summer?

The Economist

Soc. On the contrary, I know precisely that for either object, whether to bring the weeds and quitch grass to the surface and to wither them by scorching heat, or to expose the earth itself to the sun's baking rays, there can be nothing better than to plough the soil up with a pair of oxen during mid-day in midsummer.

Isch. And if a gang of men set to, to break and make this fallow with the mattock, it is transparent that their business is to separate the quitch grass from the soil and keep them parted?

Soc. Just so! —to throw the quitch grass down to wither on the surface, and to turn the soil up, so that the crude earth may have its turn of baking.

The Economist

XVII

You see, Socrates (he said, continuing the conversation), we hold the same opinion, both of us, concerning fallow.

Why, so it seems (I said)—the same opinion.

Isch. But when it comes to sowing, what is your opinion? Can you suggest a better time for sowing than that which the long experience of former generations, combined with that of men now living, recognises as the best? See, so soon as autumn time has come, the faces of all men everywhere turn with a wistful gaze towards high heaven. "When will God moisten the earth, " they ask, "and suffer men to sow their seed? "[1]

[1] See Dr. Holden's interesting note at this point: "According to Virgil ('Georg. ' i. 215), spring is the time, " etc.

Yes, Ischomachus (I answered), for all mankind must recognise the precept: [2] "Sow not on dry soil" (if it can be avoided), being taught wisdom doubtless by the heavy losses they must struggle with who sow before God's bidding.

[2] Or, "it is a maxim held of all men. "

Isch. It seems, then, you and I and all mankind hold one opinion on these matters?

Soc. Why, yes; where God himself is teacher, such accord is apt to follow; for instance, all men are agreed, it is better to wear thick clothes[3] in winter, if so be they can. We light fires by general consent, provided we have logs to burn.

[3] Or, "a thick cloak. " See Rich, s.v. Pallium (= {imation}).

Yet as regards this very period of seed-time (he made answer), Socrates, we find at once the widest difference of opinion upon one point; as to which is better, the early, or the later, [4] or the middle sowing?

[4] See Holden ad loc. Sauppe, "Lex. Xen., " notes {opsimos} as Ionic and poet. See also Rutherford, "New Phryn. " p. 124: "First met with

in a line of the 'Iliad' (ii. 325), {opsimos} does not appear till late Greek except in the 'Oeconomicus, ' a disputed work of Xenophon. "

Soc. Just so, for neither does God guide the year in one set fashion, but irregularly, now suiting it to early sowing best, and now to middle, and again to later.

Isch. But what, Socrates, is your opinion? Were it better for a man to choose and turn to sole account a single sowing season, be it much he has to sow or be it little? or would you have him begin his sowing with the earliest season, and sow right on continuously until the latest?

And I, in my turn, answered: I should think it best, Ischomachus, to use indifferently the whole sowing season. [5] Far better[6] to have enough of corn and meal at any moment and from year to year, than first a superfluity and then perhaps a scant supply.

[5] Or, "share in the entire period of seed time. " Zeune cf. "Geop. " ii. 14. 8; Mr. Ruskin's translators, "Bibl. Past. " vol. i.; cf. Eccles. xi. 6.

[6] Lit. "according to my tenet, " {nomizo}.

Isch. Then, on this point also, Socrates, you hold a like opinion with myself—the pupil to the teacher; and what is more, the pupil was the first to give it utterance.

So far, so good! (I answered). Is there a subtle art in scattering the seed?

Isch. Let us by all means investigate that point. That the seed must be cast by hand, I presume you know yourself?

Soc. Yes, by the testimony of my eyes. [7]

[7] Lit. "Yes, for I have seen it done. "

Isch. But as to actual scattering, some can scatter evenly, others cannot. [8]

[8] Holden cf. W. Harte, "Essays on Husbandry, " p. 210, 2nd ed., "The main perfection of sowing is to disperse the seeds equally. "

The Economist

Soc. Does it not come to this, the hand needs practice (like the fingers of a harp-player) to obey the will?

Isch. Precisely so, but now suppose the soil is light in one part and heavy in another?

Soc. I do not follow; by "light" do you mean weak? and by "heavy" strong?

Isch. Yes, that is what I mean. And the question which I put to you is this: Would you allow both sorts of soil an equal share of seed? or which the larger? [9]

[9] See Theophr. "Hist. Pl. " viii. 6. 2; Virg. "Georg. " ii. 275. Holden cf. Adam Dickson, "Husbandry of the Ancients, " vol. ii. 35. 33 f. (Edin. 1788), "Were the poor light land in Britain managed after the manner of the Roman husbandry, it would certainly require much less seed than under its present management. "

Soc. The stronger the wine the larger the dose of water to be added, I believe. The stronger, too, the man the heavier the weight we will lay upon his back to carry: or if it is not porterage, but people to support, there still my tenet holds: the broader and more powerful the great man's shoulders, the more mouths I should assign to him to feed. But perhaps a weak soil, like a lean pack-horse, [10] grows stronger the more corn you pour into it. This I look to you to teach me. [11]

[10] Or, "lean cattle. "

[11] Or, "Will you please answer me that question, teacher? "

With a laugh, he answered: Once more you are pleased to jest. Yet rest assured of one thing, Socrates: if after you have put seed into the ground, you will await the instant when, while earth is being richly fed from heaven, the fresh green from the hidden seed first springs, and take and turn it back again, [12] this sprouting germ will serve as food for earth: as from manure an inborn strength will presently be added to the soil. But if you suffer earth to feed the seed of corn within it and to bring forth fruit in an endless round, at last[13] it will be hard for the weakened soil to yield large corn crops, even as a weak sow can hardly rear a large litter of fat pigs.

[12] "If you will plough the seedlings in again. "

The Economist

[13] {dia telous . .. es telos}, "continually . .. in the end. " See references in Holden's fifth edition.

Soc. I understand you to say, Ischomachus, that the weaker soil must receive a scantier dose of seed?

Isch. Most decidedly I do, and you on your side, Socrates, I understand, give your consent to this opinion in stating your belief that the weaker the shoulders the lighter the burdens to be laid on them.

Soc. But those hoers with their hoes, Ischomachus, tell me for what reason you let them loose[14] upon the corn.

[14] Cf. "Revenues, " iv. 5.

Isch. You know, I daresay, that in winter there are heavy rains? [15]

[15] "And melting snows, much water every way. "

Soc. To be sure, I do.

Isch. We may suppose, then, that a portion of the corn is buried by these floods beneath a coat of mud and slime, or else that the roots are laid quite bare in places by the torrent. By reason of this same drench, I take it, oftentimes an undergrowth of weeds springs up with the corn and chokes it.

Soc. Yes, all these ills are likely enough to happen.

Isch. Are you not agreed the corn-fields sorely need relief at such a season?

Soc. Assuredly.

Isch. Then what is to be done, in your opinion? How shall we aid the stricken portion lying mud-bedabbled?

Soc. How better than by lifting up and lightening the soil?

Isch. Yes! and that other portion lying naked to the roots and defenceless, how aid it?

Soc. Possibly by mounding up fresh earth about it. [16]

[16] "Scraping up a barrier of fresh earth about it."

Isch. And what when the weeds spring up together with the corn and choke it? or when they rob and ruthlessly devour the corn's proper sustenance, like unserviceable drones[17] that rob the working bees of honey, pilfering the good food which they have made and stored away with labour: what must we do?

[17] Cf. Shakesp. "Lazy yawning drones, " "Henry V. " I. ii. 204.

Soc. In good sooth, there can be nothing for it save to cut out the noisome weed, even as drones are cleared out from the hive.

Isch. You agree there is some show of reason for letting in these gangs of hoers?

Soc. Most true. And now I am turning over in my mind, [18] Ischomachus, how grand a thing it is to introduce a simile or such like figure well and aptly. No sooner had you mentioned the word "drones" than I was filled with rage against those miserable weeds, far more than when you merely spoke of weeds and undergrowth.

[18] Or, "I was just this moment pondering the virtue of a happy illustration. " Lit. "what a thing it is to introduce an 'image' ({tas eikonas}) well. " See Plat. "Rep. " 487 E, {de eikonos}, "in a parable" (Jowett); "Phaed. " 87 B, "a figure"; Aristoph. "Clouds, " 559; Plat. "Phaedr. " 267 C; Aristot. "Rhet. " III. iv. As to the drones, J. J. Hartman, "An. X." 186, aptly cf. Aristoph. "Wasps, " 1114 f.

XVIII

But, not to interrupt you further (I continued), after sowing, naturally we hope to come to reaping. If, therefore, you have anything to say on that head also, pray proceed to teach me.

Isch. Yes, by all means, unless indeed you prove on this head also to know as much yourself already as your teacher. To begin then: You know that corn needs cutting?

Soc. To be sure, I know that much at any rate.

Isch. Well, then, the next point: in the act of cutting corn how will you choose to stand? facing the way the wind blows, [1] or against the wind?

[1] Lit. "(on the side) where the wind blows or right opposite."

Soc. Not against the wind, for my part. Eyes and hands must suffer, I imagine, if one stood reaping face to face with husks and particles of straw. [2]

[2] i. e. "with particles of straw and beards of corn blowing in one's face."

Isch. And should you merely sever the ears at top, or reap close to the ground? [3]

[3] See Holden ad loc. ; Sir Anthony Fitzherbert, "Husbandry, " 27 (ed. 1767), "In Somersetshire . .. they do share theyr wheate very lowe. . .."

If the stalk of corn were short (I answered), I should cut down close, to secure a sufficient length of straw to be of use. But if the stalk be tall, you would do right, I hold, to cut it half-way down, whereby the thresher and the winnower will be saved some extra labour (which both may well be spared). [4] The stalk left standing in the field, when burnt down (as burnt it will be, I presume), will help to benefit the soil; [5] and laid on as manure, will serve to swell the volume of manure. [6]

[4] Lit. "will be spared superfluous labour on what they do not want."

[5] Al. "if burnt down . .. ; if laid on as manure . .."

[6] "Help to swell the bulk" (Holden). For the custom see Virg. "Georg. " i. 84; J. Tull, op. cit. ix. 141: "The custom of burning the stubble on the rich plains about Rome continues to this time."

Isch. There, Socrates, you are detected "in the very act"; you know as much about reaping as I do myself.

It looks a little like it (I replied). But I would fain discover whether I have sound knowledge also about threshing.

Isch. Well, I suppose you are aware of this much: corn is threshed by beasts of burthen? [7]

[7] Holden cf. Dr. Davy, "Notes and Observations on the Ionian Islands. " "The grain is beaten out, commonly in the harvest field, by men, horses, or mules, on a threshing-floor prepared extempore for the purpose, where the ground is firm and dry, and the chaff is separated by winnowing. "—Wilkinson, "Ancient Egyptians, " ii. 41 foll.

Soc. Yes, I am aware of that much, and beast of burthen is a general name including oxen, horses, mules, and so forth. [8]

[8] See Varro, i. 52, as to tritura and ventilatio.

Isch. Is it your opinion that these animals know more than merely how to tread the corn while driven with the goad?

Soc. What more can they know, being beasts of burthen?

Isch. Some one must see, then, that the beasts tread out only what requires threshing and no more, and that the threshing is done evenly itself: to whom do you assign that duty, Socrates?

Soc. Clearly it is the duty of the threshers who are in charge. [9] It is theirs to turn the sheaves, and ever and again to push the untrodden corn under the creatures' feet; and thus, of course, to keep the threshing-floor as smooth, and finish off the work as fast, as possible.

[9] Or, "to the over-threshers, " "the drivers" (Holden).

Isch. Your comprehension of the facts thus far, it seems, keeps pace with mine.

Soc. Well, after that, Ischomachus, we will proceed to cleanse the corn by winnowing. [10]

[10] Breit. cf. Colum. "de r. r." ii. 10, 14, 21; vide Rich, s.v. ventilabrum.

Isch. Yes, but tell me, Socrates; do you know that if you begin the process from the windward portion (of the threshing-floor), you will find your chaff is carried over the whole area.

Soc. It must be so.

Isch. Then it is more than likely the chaff will fall upon the corn.

Soc. Yes, considering the distance, [11] the chaff will hardly be carried across the corn into the empty portion of the threshing-floor.

[11] Lit. "it is a long space for the chaff to be carried. " Al. (1) "It is of great consequence the chaff should be carried beyond the corn. " (2) "It often happens that the corn is blown not only on to the corn, but over and beyond it into the empty portion of the threshing-floor. " So Breit.

Isch. But now, suppose you begin winnowing on the "lee" side of the threshing-floor? [12]

[12] Or, "on the side of the threshing-floor opposite the wind. " Al. "protected from the wind. "

Soc. It is clear the chaff will at once fall into the chaff-receiver. [13]

[13] A hollowed-out portion of the threshing-floor, according to Breitenbach.

Isch. And when you have cleansed the corn over half the floor, will you proceed at once, with the corn thus strewn in front of you, to winnow the remainder, [14] or will you first pack the clean grain into the narrowest space against the central pillar? [15]

The Economist

[14] Lit. "of the chaff, " where we should say "corn, " the winnowing process separating chaff from grain and grain from chaff.

[15] If that is the meaning of {ton polon}. Al. "the outer edge or rim of the threshing-floor. "

Soc. Yes, upon my word! first pack together the clean grain, and proceed. My chaff will now be carried into the empty portion of the floor, and I shall escape the need of winnowing twice over. [16]

[16] Or, "the same chaff (i. e. unwinnowed corn, Angl. corn) twice. "

Isch. Really, Socrates, you are fully competent yourself, it seems, to teach an ignorant world[17] the speediest mode of winnowing.

[17] Lit. "After all, Socrates, it seems you could even teach another how to purge his corn most expeditiously. "

Soc. It seems, then, as you say, I must have known about these matters, though unconsciously; and here I stand and beat my brains, [18] reflecting whether or not I may not know some other things — how to refine gold and play the flute and paint pictures—without being conscious of the fact. Certainly, as far as teaching goes, no one ever taught me these, no more than husbandry; while, as to using my own eyes, I have watched men working at the other arts no less than I have watched them till the soil.

[18] Lit. "all this while, I am thinking whether . .. "

Isch. Did I not tell you long ago that of all arts husbandry was the noblest, the most generous, just because it is the easiest to learn?

Soc. That it is without a doubt, Ischomachus. It seems I must have known the processes of sowing, without being conscious of my knowledge. [19]

[19] Or, "but for all my science, I was ignorant (of knowing my own knowledge). "

XIX

Soc. (continuing). But may I ask, is the planting of trees[1] a department in the art of husbandry?

[1] i. e. of fruit trees, the vine, olive, fig, etc.

Isch. Certainly it is.

Soc. How is it, then, that I can know about the processes of sowing and at the same time have no knowledge about planting?

Isch. Is it so certain that you have no knowledge?

Soc. How can you ask me? when I neither know the sort of soil in which to plant, nor yet the depth of hole[2] the plant requires, nor the breadth, or length of ground in which it needs to be embedded; [3] nor lastly, how to lay the plant in earth, with any hope of fostering its growth. [4]

[2] Reading {to phuto}, "nor yet how deep or broad to sink (the hole) for the plant. " Holden (ed. 1886) supplies {bothunon}. Al. {bothron}.

[3] See Loudon, "Encycl. of Agric. " S. 407, ap. Holden: "In France plantations of the vine are made by dibbling in cuttings of two feet of length; pressing the earth firmly to their lower end, an essential part of the operation, noticed even by Xenophon. "

[4] Lit. "how, laid in the soil, the plant will best shoot forth or grow. "

Isch. Come, then, to lessons, pupil, and be taught whatever you do not know already! You have seen, I know, the sort of trenches which are dug for plants?

Soc. Hundreds of times.

Isch. Did you ever see one more than three feet deep?

Soc. No, I do not think I ever saw one more than two and a half feet deep.

The Economist

Isch. Well, as to the breadth now. Did you ever see a trench more than three feet broad? [5]

[5] Or, "width, " "wide. " The commentators cf. Plin. "H. N." xvii. 11, 16, 22; Columell. v. 5. 2; ib. iii. 15. 2; Virg. "Georg. " ii. 288.

Soc. No, upon my word, not even more than two feet broad.

Isch. Good! now answer me this question: Did you ever see a trench less than one foot deep?

Soc. No, indeed! nor even less than one foot and a half. Why, the plants would be no sooner buried than dug out again, if planted so extremely near the surface.

Isch. Here, then, is one matter, Socrates, which you know as well as any one. [6] The trench is not to be sunk deeper than two feet and a half, or shallower than one foot and a half.

[6] Lit. "quite adequately. "

Soc. Obviously, a thing so plain appeals to the eye at once.

Isch. Can you by eyesight recognise the difference between a dry soil and a moist?

Soc. I should certainly select as dry the soil round Lycabettus, [7] and any that resembles it; and as moist, the soil in the marsh meadows of Phalerum, [8] or the like.

[7] See Leake, "Topog. of Athens, " i. 209.

[8] Or, "the Phaleric marsh-land. " See Leake, ib. 231, 427; ii. 9.

Isch. In planting, would you dig (what I may call) deep trenches in a dry soil or a moist?

Soc. In a dry soil certainly; at any rate, if you set about to dig deep trenches in the moist you will come to water, and there and then an end to further planting.

Isch. You could not put it better. We will suppose, then, the trenches have been dug. Does your eyesight take you further? [9] Have you

The Economist

noticed at what season in either case[10] the plants must be embedded?

[9] Lit. "As soon as the trenches have been dug then, have you further noticed . . . "

[10] (1) The vulg. reading {openika . .. ekatera} = "at what precise time . .. either (i. e. 'the two different' kinds of) plant, " i. e. "vine and olive" or "vine and fig, " I suppose; (2) Breit. emend. {opotera . .. en ekatera} = "which kind of plant . .. in either soil . .. "; (3) Schenkl. etc., {openika . .. en ekatera} = "at what season . .. in each of the two sorts of soil . .. "

Soc. Certainly. [11]

[11] There is an obvious lacuna either before or after this remark, or at both places.

Isch. Supposing, then, you wish the plants to grow as fast as possible: how will the cutting strike and sprout, do you suppose, most readily? —after you have laid a layer of soil already worked beneath it, and it merely has to penetrate soft mould? or when it has to force its way through unbroken soil into the solid ground?

Soc. Clearly it will shoot through soil which has been worked more quickly than through unworked soil.

Isch. Well then, a bed of earth must be laid beneath the plant?

Soc. I quite agree; so let it be.

Isch. And how do you expect your cutting to root best? —if set straight up from end to end, pointing to the sky? [12] or if you set it slantwise under its earthy covering, so as to lie like an inverted gamma? [13]

[12] Lit. "if you set the whole cutting straight up, facing heavenwards. "

[13] i. e. Anglice, "like the letter {G} upon its back" {an inverted "upper-case" gamma looks like an L}. See Lord Bacon, "Nat. Hist. " Cent. v. 426: "When you would have many new roots of fruit-trees, take a low tree and bow it and lay all his branches aflat upon the

The Economist

ground and cast earth upon them; and every twig will take root. And this is a very profitable experiment for costly trees (for the boughs will make stock without charge), such as are apricots, peaches, almonds, cornelians, mulberries, figs, etc. The like is continually practised with vines, roses, musk roses, etc. "

Soc. Like an inverted gamma, to be sure, for so the plant must needs have more eyes under ground. Now it is from these same eyes of theirs, if I may trust my own, [14] that plants put forth their shoots above ground. I imagine, therefore, the eyes still underground will do the same precisely, and with so many buds all springing under earth, the plant itself, I argue, as a whole will sprout and shoot and push its way with speed and vigour.

[14] Lit. "it is from their eyes, I see, that plants . .. "

Isch. I may tell you that on these points, too, your judgment tallies with my own. But now, should you content yourself with merely heaping up the earth, or will you press it firmly round your plant?

Soc. I should certainly press down the earth; for if the earth is not pressed down, I know full well that at one time under the influence of rain the unpressed soil will turn to clay or mud; at another, under the influence of the sun, it will turn to sand or dust to the very bottom: so that the poor plant runs a risk of being first rotted with moisture by the rain, and next of being shrivelled up with drought through overheating of the roots. [15]

[15] Through "there being too much bottom heat. " Holden (ed. 1886).

Isch. So far as the planting of vines is concerned, it appears, Socrates, that you and I again hold views precisely similar.

And does this method of planting apply also to the fig-tree? (I inquired).

Isch. Surely, and not to the fig-tree alone, but to all the rest of fruit-trees. [16] What reason indeed would there be for rejecting in the case of other plant-growths[17] what is found to answer so well with the vine?

[16] {akrodrua} = "edible fruits" in Xenophon's time. See Plat. "Criti. " 115 B; Dem. "c. Nicostr. " 1251; Aristot. "Hist. An. " viii. 28. 8, {out akrodrua out opora khronios}; Theophr. "H. Pl. " iv. 4. 11. (At a later period, see "Geopon. " x. 74, = "fruits having a hard rind or shell, " e. g. nuts, acorns, as opposed to pears, apples, grapes, etc., {opora}.) See further the interesting regulations in Plat. "Laws, " 844 D, 845 C.

[17] Lit. "planting in general. "

Soc. How shall we plant the olive, pray, Ischomachus?

Isch. I see your purpose. You ask that question with a view to put me to the test, [18] when you know the answer yourself as well as possible. You can see with your own eyes[19] that the olive has a deeper trench dug, planted as it is so commonly by the side of roads. You can see that all the young plants in the nursery adhere to stumps. [20] And lastly, you can see that a lump of clay is placed on the head of every plant, [21] and the portion of the plant above the soil is protected by a wrapping. [22]

[18] Plat. "Prot. " 311 B, 349 C; "Theaet. " 157 C: "I cannot make out whether you are giving your own opinion, or only wanting to draw me out" (Jowett).

[19] For the advantage, see "Geopon. " iii. 11. 2.

[20] Holden cf. Virg. "Georg. " ii. 30—

quin et caudicibus sectis, mirabile dictu, truditur e sicco radix oleagina ligno.

The stock in slices cut, and forth shall shoot, O passing strange! from each dry slice a root (Holden).

See John Martyn ad loc. : "La Cerda says, that what the Poet here speaks of was practised in Spain in his time. They take the trunk of an olive, says he, deprive it of its root and branches, and cut it into several pieces, which they put into the ground, whence a root and, soon afterwards, a tree is formed. " This mode of propagating by dry pieces of the trunk (with bark on) is not to be confounded with that of "truncheons" mentioned in "Georg. " ii. 63.

[21] See Theophr. "H. Pl. " ii. 2, 4; "de Caus. " iii. 5. 1; "Geopon. " ix. 11. 4, ap. Hold. ; Col. v. 9. 1; xi. 2. 42.

[22] Or, "covered up for protection. "

Soc. Yes, all these things I see.

Isch. Granted, you see: what is there in the matter that you do not understand? Perhaps you are ignorant how you are to lay the potsherd on the clay at top?

Soc. No, in very sooth, not ignorant of that Ischomachus, or anything you mentioned. That is just the puzzle, and again I beat my brains to discover why, when you put to me that question a while back: "Had I, in brief, the knowledge how to plant? " I answered, "No. " Till then it never would have struck me that I could say at all how planting must be done. But no sooner do you begin to question me on each particular point than I can answer you; and what is more, my answers are, you tell me, accordant with the views of an authority[23] at once so skilful and so celebrated as yourself. Really, Ischomachus, I am disposed to ask: "Does teaching consist in putting questions? "[24] Indeed, the secret of your system has just this instant dawned upon me. I seem to see the principle in which you put your questions. You lead me through the field of my own knowledge, [25] and then by pointing out analogies[26] to what I know, persuade me that I really know some things which hitherto, as I believed, I had no knowledge of.

[23] Or, "whose skill in farming is proverbial. "

[24] Lit. "Is questioning after all a kind of teaching? " See Plat. "Meno"; "Mem. " IV. vi. 15.

[25] It appears, then, that the Xenophontean Socrates has {episteme} of a sort.

[26] Or, "a series of resemblances, " "close parallels, " reading {epideiknus}: or if with Breit. {apodeiknus}, transl. "by proving such or such a thing is like some other thing known to me already. "

Isch. Do you suppose if I began to question you concerning money and its quality, [27] I could possibly persuade you that you know the method to distinguish good from false coin? Or could I, by a string of

The Economist

questions about flute-players, painters, and the like, induce you to believe that you yourself know how to play the flute, or paint, and so forth?

[27] Lit. "whether it is good or not."

Soc. Perhaps you might; for have you not persuaded me I am possessed of perfect knowledge of this art of husbandry, [28] albeit I know that no one ever taught this art to me?

[28] Or, "since you actually succeeded in persuading me I was scientifically versed in," etc. See Plat. "Statesm." 301 B; "Theaet." 208 E; Aristot. "An. Post." i. 6. 4; "Categ." 8. 41.

Isch. Ah! that is not the explanation, Socrates. The truth is what I told you long ago and kept on telling you. Husbandry is an art so gentle, so humane, that mistress-like she makes all those who look on her or listen to her voice intelligent[29] of herself at once. Many a lesson does she herself impart how best to try conclusions with her. [30] See, for instance, how the vine, making a ladder of the nearest tree whereon to climb, informs us that it needs support. [31] Anon it spreads its leaves when, as it seems to say, "My grapes are young, my clusters tender," and so teaches us, during that season, to screen and shade the parts exposed to the sun's rays; but when the appointed moment comes, when now it is time for the swelling clusters to be sweetened by the sun, behold, it drops a leaf and then a leaf, so teaching us to strip it bare itself and let the vintage ripen. With plenty teeming, see the fertile mother shows her mellow clusters, and the while is nursing a new brood in primal crudeness. [32] So the vine plant teaches us how best to gather in the vintage, even as men gather figs, the juiciest first. [33]

[29] Or, "gives them at once a perfect knowledge of herself."

[30] Lit. "best to deal with her," "make use of her."

[31] Lit. "teaches us to prop it."

[32] Lit. "yet immature."

[33] Or, "first one and then another as it swells. " Cf. Shakespeare:

The mellow plum doth fall, the green sticks fast, Or being early pluck'd is sour to taste ("V. and A. " 527).

The Economist

XX

At this point in the conversation I remarked: Tell me, Ischomachus, if the details of the art of husbandry are thus easy to learn, and all alike know what needs to be done, how does it happen that all farmers do not fare like, but some live in affluence owning more than they can possibly enjoy, while others of them fail to obtain the barest necessities and actually run into debt?

I will tell you, Socrates (Ischomachus replied). It is neither knowledge nor lack of knowledge in these husbandmen which causes some to be well off, while others are in difficulties; nor will you ever hear such tales afloat as that this or that estate has gone to ruin because the sower failed to sow evenly, or that the planter failed to plant straight rows of plants, or that such an one, [1] being ignorant what soil was best suited to bear vines, had set his plants in sterile ground, or that another[2] was in ignorance that fallow must be broken up for purposes of sowing, or that a third[3] was not aware that it is good to mix manure in with the soil. No, you are much more likely to hear said of So-and-so: No wonder the man gets in no wheat from his farm, when he takes no pains to have it sown or properly manured. Or of some other that he grows no wine: Of course not, when he takes no pains either to plant new vines or to make those he has bear fruit. A third has neither figs nor olives; and again the self-same reason: He too is careless, and takes no steps whatever to succeed in growing either one or other. These are the distinctions which make all the difference to prosperity in farming, far more than the reputed discovery of any clever agricultural method or machine. [4]

[1] "Squire This."

[2] "Squire That."

[3] "Squire T'other."

[4] There is something amiss with the text at this point. For emendations see Breit., Schenkl, Holden, Hartman.

You will find the principle applies elsewhere. There are points of strategic conduct in which generals differ from each other for the better or the worse, not because they differ in respect of wit or judgment, but of carefulness undoubtedly. I speak of things within the cognisance of every general, and indeed of almost every private soldier, which some commanders are careful to perform and others not. Who does not know, for instance, that in marching through a hostile territory an army ought to march in the order best adapted to deliver battle with effect should need arise? [5]—a golden rule which, punctually obeyed by some, is disobeyed by others. Again, as all the world knows, it is better to place day and night pickets[6] in front of an encampment. Yet even that is a procedure which, carefully observed at times, is at times as carelessly neglected. Once more: not one man in ten thousand, [7] I suppose, but knows that when a force is marching through a narrow defile, the safer method is to occupy beforehand certain points of vantage. [8] Yet this precaution also has been known to be neglected.

[5] See Thuc. ii. 81: "The Hellenic troops maintained order on the march and kept a look-out until . .. "—Jowett.

[6] See "Cyrop. " I. vi. 43.

[7] Lit. "it would be hard to find the man who did not know. "

[8] Or, "to seize advantageous positions in advance. " Cf. "Hiero, " x. 5.

Similarly, every one will tell you that manure is the best thing in the world for agriculture, and every one can see how naturally it is produced. Still, though the method of production is accurately known, though there is every facility to get it in abundance, the fact remains that, while one man takes pains to have manure collected, another is entirely neglectful. And yet God sends us rain from heaven, and every hollow place becomes a standing pool, while earth supplies materials of every kind; the sower, too, about to sow must cleanse the soil, and what he takes as refuse from it needs only to be thrown into water and time itself will do the rest, shaping all to gladden earth. [9] For matter in every shape, nay earth itself, [10] in stagnant water turns to fine manure.

[9] Lit. "Time itself will make that wherein Earth rejoices. "

[10] i. e. "each fallen leaf, each sprig or spray of undergrowth, the very weeds, each clod. " Lit. "what kind of material, what kind of soil does not become manure when thrown into stagnant water? "

The Economist

So, again, as touching the various ways in which the earth itself needs treatment, either as being too moist for sowing, or too salt[11] for planting, these and the processes of cure are known to all men: how in one case the superfluous water is drawn off by trenches, and in the other the salt corrected by being mixed with various non-salt bodies, moist or dry. Yet here again, in spite of knowledge, some are careful of these matters, others negligent.

[11] See Anatol. "Geop. " ii. 10. 9; Theophr. "de Caus. " ii. 5. 4, 16. 8, ap. Holden. Cf. Virg. "Georg. " ii. 238:

salsa autem tellus, et quae perhibetur amara frugibus infelix.

But even if a man were altogether ignorant what earth can yield, were he debarred from seeing any fruit or plant, prevented hearing from the lips of any one the truth about this earth: even so, I put it to you, it would be easier far for any living soul to make experiments on a piece of land, [12] than on a horse, for instance, or on his fellow-man. For there is nought which earth displays with intent to deceive, but in clear and simple language stamped with the seal of truth she informs us what she can and cannot do. [13] Thus it has ever seemed to me that earth is the best discoverer of true honesty, [14] in that she offers all her stores of knowledge in a shape accessible to the learner, so that he who runs may read. Here it is not open to the sluggard, as in other arts, to put forward the plea of ignorance or lack of knowledge, for all men know that earth, if kindly treated, will repay in kind. No! there is no witness[15] against a coward soul so clear as that of husbandry; [16] since no man ever yet persuaded himself that he could live without the staff of life. He therefore that is unskilled in other money-making arts and will not dig, shows plainly he is minded to make his living by picking and stealing, or by begging alms, or else he writes himself down a very fool. [17]

[12] Or, "this fair earth herself. "

[13] Or, "earth our mother reveals her powers and her impotence. "

[14] Lit. "of the good and the bad. " Cf. Dem. "adv. Phorm. " 918. 18.

[15] Lit. "no accuser of. " Cf. Aesch. "Theb. " 439.

[16] Reading, with Sauppe, {all' e georgia}, or if, with Jacobs, {e en georgia argia}, transl. "as that of idleness in husbandry. "

The Economist

[17] Or, "if not, he must be entirely irrational. " Cf. Plat. "Apol. " 37 C.

Presently, Ischomachus proceeded: Now it is of prime importance, [18] in reference to the profitableness or unprofitableness of agriculture, even on a large estate where there are numerous[19] workfolk, [20] whether a man takes any pains at all to see that his labourers are devoted to the work on hand during the appointed time, [21] or whether he neglects that duty. Since one man will fairly distance ten[22] simply by working at the time, and another may as easily fall short by leaving off before the hour. [23] In fact, to let the fellows take things easily the whole day through will make a difference easily of half in the whole work. [24]

[18] Lit. "it made a great difference, he said, with regard to profit and loss in agriculture. "

[19] Or if, after Hertlein, adding {kai meionon}, transl. "workmen now more, now less, in number. "

[20] {ergasteron}, "poet. " L. & S. cf. "Orph. H." 65. 4. See above, v. 15; xiii. 10.

[21] Cf. Herod. II. ii. 2.

[22] Or, "Why! one man in ten makes all the difference by . .. " {para} = "by comparison with. "

[23] Reading as vulg., or if {to me pro k. t.l. } transl. "by not leaving off, etc. "

[24] i. e. "is a difference of fifty per cent on the whole work. "

As, on a walking-expedition, it may happen, of two wayfarers, the one will gain in pace upon the other half the distance say in every five- and-twenty miles, [25] though both alike are young and hale of body. The one, in fact, is bent on compassing the work on which he started, he steps out gaily and unflinchingly; the other, more slack in spirit, stops to recruit himself and contemplate the view by fountain side and shady nook, as though his object were to court each gentle zephyr. So in farm work; there is a vast difference as regards performance between those who do it not, but seek excuse for idleness and are suffered to be listless. Thus, between good honest work and base neglect there is as great a difference as there is between—what shall I say? —why, work and idleness. [26] The gardeners, look, are hoeing vines to keep them clean and free of weeds; but they hoe so sorrily that the loose stuff grows ranker and more plentiful. Can you call that[27] anything but idleness?

[25] Lit. "per 200 stades. "

[26] Or, "wholly to work and wholly to be idle. " Reading as Sauppe, etc., or if with Holden, etc., {to de de kalos kai to kakos ergazesthai e epimeleisthai}, transl. "between toil and carefulness well or ill expended there lies all the difference; the two things are sundered as wide apart as are the poles of work and play, " etc. A. Jacobs' emend. ap. Hartm. "An. Xen. " p. 211, {to de de kakos ergazesthai e kakos epimeleisthai kei to kalos}, seems happy.

[27] Or, "such a hoer aught but an idle loon. "

Such, Socrates, are the ills which cause a house to crumble far more than lack of scientific knowledge, however rude it be. [28] For if you will consider; on the one hand, there is a steady outflow[29] of expenses from the house, and, on the other, a lack of profitable works outside to meet expenses; need you longer wonder if the field-works create a deficit and not a surplus? In proof, however, that the man who can give the requisite heed, while straining every nerve in the pursuit of agriculture, has speedy[30] and effective means of making money, I may cite the instance of my father, who had practised what he preached. [31]

[28] Cf. Thuc. v. 7; Plat. "Rep. " 350 A; "Theaet. " 200 B.

[29] Or, "the expenses from the house are going on at the full rate, " {enteleis}. Holden cf. Aristoph. "Knights, " 1367: {ton misthon apodoso 'ntele}, "I'll have the arrears of seamen's wages paid to a penny" (Frere).

[30] {anutikotaten}. Cf. "Hipparch, " ii. 6.

[31] Or, "who merely taught me what he had himself carried out in practice. "

Now, my father would never suffer me to purchase an estate already under cultivation, but if he chanced upon a plot of land which, owing to the neglect or incapacity of the owner, was neither tilled nor planted, [32] nothing would satisfy him but I must purchase it. He had a saying that estates already under cultivation cost a deal of money and allowed of no improvement; and where there is no prospect of improvement, more than half the pleasure to be got from the possession vanishes. The height of happiness was, he maintained, to see your purchase, be it dead chattel or live animal, [33] go on improving daily under your own eyes. [34] Now, nothing shows a larger increase[35] than a piece of land reclaimed from barren waste and bearing fruit a hundredfold. I can assure you, Socrates, many is the farm which my father and I made worth I do not know how many times more than its original value. And then, Socrates, this valuable invention[36] is so easy to learn that you who have but heard it know and understand it as well as I myself do, and can go away and teach it to another if you choose. Yet my father did not learn it of another, nor did he discover it by a painful mental process; [37] but, as he has often told me, through pure love of husbandry and fondness of toil, he would become enamoured of such a spot as I describe, [38] and then nothing would content him but he must own it, in order to have something to do, and at the same time, to derive pleasure along with profit from the purchase. For you must know, Socrates, of all Athenians I have ever heard of, my father, as it seems to me, had the greatest love for agricultural pursuits.

[32] i. e. out of cultivation, whether as corn land or for fruit trees, viz. olive, fig, vine, etc.

[33] Or, "be it a dead thing or a live pet. " Cf. Plat. "Theaet. " 174 B; "Laws, " 789 B, 790 D, 819 B; "C. I." 1709.

[34] Cf. "Horsem. " iii. 1; and see Cowley's Essay above referred to.

[35] Or, "is susceptible of greater improvement. "

[36] Or, "discovery. " See "Anab. " III. v. 12; "Hell. " IV. v. 4; "Hunting, " xiii. 13.

[37] Or, "nor did he rack his brains to discover it. " See "Mem. " III. v. 23. Cf. Aristoph. "Clouds, " 102, {merimnophrontistai}, minute philosophers.

[38] "He could not see an estate of the sort described but he must fall over head and ears in love with it at first sight; have it he must."

When I heard this, I could not resist asking a question; Ischomachus (I said), did your father retain possession of all the farms he put under cultivation, or did he part with them whenever he was offered a good price?

He parted with them, without a doubt (replied Ischomachus), but then at once he bought another in the place of what he sold, and in every case an untilled farm, in order to gratify his love for owrk.

As you describe him (I proceeded), your father must truly have been formed by nature with a passion for husbandry, not unlike that corn-hunger which merchants suffer from. You know their habits: by reason of this craving after corn, [39] whenever they hear that corn is to be got, they go sailing off to find it, even if they must cross the Aegean, or the Euxine, or the Sicilian seas. And when they have got as much as ever they can get, they will not let it out of their sight, but store it in the vessel on which they sail themselves, and off they go across the seas again. [40] Whenever they stand in need of money, they will not discharge their precious cargo, [41] at least not in haphazard fashion, wherever they may chance to be; but first they find out where corn is at the highest value, and where the inhabitants will set the greatest store by it, and there they take and deliver the dear article. Your father's fondness for agriculture seems to bear a certain family resemblance to this passion.

[39] Lit. "of their excessive love for corn."

[40] Lit. "they carry it across the seas again, and that, too, after having stored it in the hold of the very vessel in which they sail themselves."

[41] Or, "their treasure." {auton} throughout, which indeed is the humour of the passage. The love of John Barleycorn is their master passion.

To these remarks Ischomachus replied: You jest, Socrates; but still I hold to my belief: that man is fond of bricks and mortar who no sooner has built one house than he must needs sell it and proceed to build another.

The Economist

To be sure, Ischomachus (I answered), and for my part I assure you, upon oath, I, Socrates, do verily and indeed believe[42] you that all men by nature love (or hold they ought to love) those things wherebysoever they believe they will be benefited.

[32] Reading {e men pisteuein soi phusei (nomizein) philein tauta pantas . .. }; and for the "belief" propounded with so much humorous emphasis, see Adam Smith, "Moral Sentiments. " Hartman, "An. Xen. " 180, cf. Plat. "Lysis. "

The Economist

XXI

After a pause, I added: I am turning over in my mind how cleverly you have presented the whole argument to support your thesis: which was, that of all arts the art of husbandry is the easiest to learn. And now, as the result of all that has been stated, I am entirely persuaded that this is so.

Isch. Yes, Socrates, indeed it is. But I, on my side, must in turn admit that as regards that faculty which is common alike to every kind of conduct (tillage, or politics, the art of managing a house, or of conducting war), the power, namely, of command[1]—I do subscribe to your opinion, that on this score one set of people differ largely from another both in point of wit and judgement. On a ship of war, for instance, [2] the ship is on the high seas, and the crew must row whole days together to reach moorings. [3] Now note the difference. Here you may find a captain[4] able by dint of speech and conduct to whet the souls of those he leads, and sharpen them to voluntary toils; and there another so dull of wit and destitute of feeling that it will take his crew just twice the time to finish the same voyage. See them step on shore. The first ship's company are drenched in sweat; but listen, they are loud in praise of one another, the captain and his merry men alike. And the others? They are come at last; they have not turned a hair, the lazy fellows, but for all that they hate their officer and by him are hated.

[1] See "Mem. " I. i. 7.

[2] Or, "the crew must row the livelong day . . . "

[3] For an instance see "Hell. " VI. ii. 27, Iphicrates' periplus.

[4] Or, "one set of boatswains. " See Thuc. ii. 84. For the duties of the Keleustes see "Dict. Gk. Rom. Ant. " s. v. portisculus; and for the type of captain see "Hell. " V. i. 3, Teleutias.

Generals, too, will differ (he proceeded), the one sort from the other, in this very quality. Here you have a leader who, incapable of kindling a zest for toil and love of hairbreadth 'scapes, is apt to engender in his followers that base spirit which neither deigns nor chooses to obey, except under compulsion. They even pride and plume themselves, [5] the cowards, on their opposition to their leader; this same leader who, in the end, will make his men insensible to shame even in presence of most foul mishap. On the other hand, put at their head another stamp of general: one who is by right divine[6] a leader, good and brave, a man of scientific knowledge. Let him take over to his charge those malcontents, or others even of worse character, and he will have them presently ashamed of doing a disgraceful deed. "It is nobler to obey" will be their maxim. They will exult in personal obedience and in common toil, where toil is needed, cheerily performed. For just as an unurged zeal for voluntary service[7] may at times invade, we know, the breasts of private soldiers, so may like love of toil with emulous longing to achieve great deeds of valour under the eyes of their commander, be implanted in whole armies by good officers.

[5] Lit. "magnify themselves. " See "Ages. " x. 2; "Pol. Lac. " viii. 2.

[6] Or, "god-like, " "with something more than human in him. " See Hom. "Il. " xxiv. 259:

{oude eokei andros ge thnetou pais emmenai alla theoio. }

"Od. " iv. 691; {theioi basilees}. Cf. Carlyle, "Heroes"; Plat. "Meno, " 99 D: Soc. "And may we not, Meno, truly call those men divine who, having no understanding, yet succeed in many a grand deed and word? " And below: Soc. "And the women too, Meno, call good men divine; and the Spartans, when they praise a good man, say, 'that he is a divine man'" (Jowett). Arist. "Eth. N." vii. 1: "That virtue which transcends the human, and which is of an heroic or godlike type, such as Priam, in the poems of Homer, ascribes to Hector, when wishing to speak of his great goodness:

Not woman-born seemed he, but sprung from gods. "

And below: "And exactly as it is a rare thing to find a man of godlike nature—to use the expression of the Spartans, 'a godlike man, ' which they apply to those whom they expressively admire—so, too, brutality is a type of character rarely found among men" (Robert Williams).

[7] Reading {etheloponia tis}, or if {philoponia}, transl. "just as some strange delight in labour may quicken in the heart of many an individual soldier. " See "Anab. " IV. vii. 11.

The Economist

Happy must that leader be whose followers are thus attached to him: beyond all others he will prove a stout and strong commander. And by strong, I mean, not one so hale of body as to tower above the stoutest of the soldiery themselves; no, nor him whose skill to hurl a javelin or shoot an arrow will outshine the skilfullest; nor yet that mounted on the fleetest charger it shall be his to bear the brunt of danger foremost amid the knightliest horsemen, the nimblest of light infantry. No, not these, but who is able to implant a firm persuasion in the minds of all his soldiers: follow him they must and will through fire, if need be, or into the jaws of death. [8]

[8] Or, "through flood and fire or other desperate strait. " Cf. "Anab. " II. vi. 8.

Lofty of soul and large of judgment[9] may he be designated justly, at whose back there steps a multitude stirred by his sole sentiment; not unreasonably may he be said to march "with a mighty arm, "[10] to whose will a thousand willing hands are prompt to minister; a great man in every deed he is who can achieve great ends by resolution rather than brute force.

[9] See "Ages. " ix. 6, "of how lofty a sentiment. "

[10] See Herod. vii. 20, 157; Thuc. iii. 96.

So, too, within the field of private industry, the person in authority, be it the bailiff, be it the overseer, [11] provided he is able to produce unflinching energy, intense and eager, for the work, belongs to those who haste to overtake good things[12] and reap great plenty. Should the master (he proceeded), being a man possessed of so much power, Socrates, to injure the bad workman and reward the zealous — should he suddenly appear, and should his appearance in the labour field produce no visible effect upon his workpeople, I cannot say I envy or admire him. But if the sight of him is followed by a stir of movement, if there come upon[13] each labourer fresh spirit, with mutual rivaly and keen ambition, drawing out the finest qualities of each, [14] of him I should say, Behold a man of kingly disposition. And this, if I mistake not, is the quality of greatest import in every operation which needs the instrumentality of man; but most of all, perhaps, in agriculture. Not that I would maintain that it is a thing to be lightly learnt by a glance of the eye, or hearsay fashion, as a tale that is told. Far from it, I assert that he who is to have this power has need of education; he must have at bottom a good natural disposition; and, what is greatest of all, he must be himself a godlike being. [15] For if I rightly understand this blessed gift, this faculty of command over willing followers, by no means is it, in its entirety, a merely human quality, but it is in part divine. It is a gift plainly given to those truly initiated[16] in the mystery of self-command. Whereas despotism over unwilling slaves, the heavenly ones give, as it seems to me, to those whom they deem worthy to live the life of Tantalus in Hades, of whom it is written[17] "he consumes unending days in apprehension of a second death. "

[11] According to Sturz, "Lex. " s. v., the {epitropos} is (as a rule, see "Mem. " II. viii.) a slave or freedman, the {epistates} a free man. See "Mem. " III. v. 18.

[12] Apparently a homely formula, like "make hay whilst the sun shines, " "a stitch in time saves nine. "

[13] Cf. Hom. "Il. " ix. 436, xvii. 625; "Hell. " VII. i. 31.

[14] Reading {kratiste ousa}, or if with Heindorf, {kratisteusai}, transl. "to prove himself the best. "

[15] See "Cyrop. " I. i. 3; Grote, "Plato, " vol. iii. 571.

[16] See Plat. "Phaed. " 69 C; Xen. "Symp. " i. 10.

[17] Or, "it is said. " See Eur. "Orest. " 5, and Porson ad loc.

Grindhouse Nostalgia